THE LAST ENEMY

Preparing to Win
the Fight of Your Life

MICHAEL E. WITTMER

DISCOVERY HOUSE
P U B L I S H E R S®

Feeding the Soul with the Word of God

Discovery House is affiliated with RBC Ministries, Grand Rapids, Michigan.

Requests for permission to quote from this book should be directed to: Permissions Department, Discovery House Publishers, P.O. Box 3566, Grand Rapids, MI 49501, or contact us by e-mail at permissionsdept@ dhp.org

Interior design by Melissa Elenbaas

Library of Congress Cataloging-in-Publication Data

Wittmer, Michael Eugene.
The last enemy : preparing to win the fight of your life / Michael E. Wittmer.
   p. cm.
ISBN 978-1-57293-514-3
1. Spiritual warfare. I. Title.
BV4509.5.W59 2012
236'.1–dc23

2011043753

Printed in the United States of America

First printing in 2012

"Though death is a cold subject, there is no need to cringe at the thought of reading this warm book. With *The Last Enemy*, Dr. Wittmer places a pastoral hand on our shoulders and shows us how with 'shaky knees and sweaty palms, faith swallows hard and clings to God's promise that we will live again.' Here is a book that is accessible to all readers but also theologically sound. And since, until Christ returns, the death rate will be right around 100 percent, we all need to prepare for our final breath with just such a book as this. *The Last Enemy* is a book that I will regularly recommend and give away."

Dr. Chris Brauns, author of *Unpacking Forgiveness*
Pastor, The Red Brick Church, Stillman Valley, IL

"Need a recipe for a great book? Start with a topic of desperate relevance. We all face death. Add a writer who makes it look easy to write engaging, accessible, sophisticated theology. Who better than Mike Wittmer? The secret, though, to this recipe is the glorious truth that Christ has conquered death. This may sound strange, but as unpleasant as it may be to think about death, Wittmer's joy in Christ makes this a fun book to read."

James Hamilton
Author of *God's Glory in Salvation through Judgment*
Associate Professor of Biblical Theology, Southern Baptist
Theological Seminary

"When you are young you feel bulletproof—life is long and death is a distant non-reality. And then you stand by the casket of a friend whose life was extinguished suddenly or you start getting old and can see your mortality quickly approaching on the horizon. There are reminders all around us that death is the ever-present, not-so-far-away enemy that threatens to take all the fun out of living. Someone needs to help us understand this haunting shadow—and not with worn out platitudes! Not to my surprise, Mike Wittmer is the one whose pen flows with honest and transparent reflections on how to get the 'exit ramp from life' into a productive perspective. This is the book that all of us need to read so that we can look forward to the fatal moment with courage, confidence, and eager anticipation!"

Dr. Joseph M. Stowell
Author of *Eternity: Reclaiming a Passion for What Endures*
President, Cornerstone University

"Everyone who plans to die should read this honest look at our enemy. Each candid chapter is as plain and unadorned as Mike Wittmer the man can be—and he really can be that. But the logic is also strong with Mike Wittmer the theologian's biblical understanding. And that offers courage without clichés. Plan to read it!"

Knute Larson, author of *The Great Human Race*
Pastor emeritus, The Chapel, Akron, OH

"Michael Wittmer has done a powerful service to those facing their own death with this helpful book. He replaces the shallow platitudes of pop religion with Holy Scripture's clear teachings about life, death, and eternal life. Michael illustrates in refreshing manner why we can die and still live in Jesus Christ, death's Conqueror. Hope and humor make this book a powerful resource for a tough time. I heartily recommend it!"

Rev. Robert Deardoff
Pastor, Beautiful Savior Lutheran Church,
North Platte, NE

For Abe and Mary Yoder,
helper of the fatherless (Psalm 10:14).
You graced my life before I was born;
we are your legacy.

CONTENTS

ACKNOWLEDGMENTS

NOTHING WORTHWHILE IS EVER accomplished alone, and that is true of this book. I am indebted to Carol Holquist and Judith Markham, who shared my vision for this project, and Miranda Gardner, who expertly and winsomely edited the manuscript. I also benefited from readers who shared insights on early drafts, including Jonathan Shelley, Joyce Clark, and my dear wife, Julie.

Julie, if I had to do it over again, I'd marry you. And we'd have three children, Avery, Landon, and Alayna, who love the Lord and each other. Our lives are so full this time around; imagine how much fun we'll have when Jesus returns!

PART ONE

KNOW YOUR ENEMY

ONE

SHOCK

What man can live and not see death, or save himself from the power of the grave?

Psalm 89:48

YOU ARE GOING TO DIE. Take a moment to let that sink in. You are going to *die*. One morning the sun will rise and you won't see it. Birds will greet the dawn and you won't hear them. Friends and family will gather to celebrate your life, and after you're buried they'll return to the church for ham and scalloped potatoes. Soon your job and favorite chair and spot on the team will be filled by someone else. The rest of the world may pause to remember—it will give you a moment of silence if you were rich or well known—but then it will carry on as it did before you arrived. "There is no remembrance of men of old," observed Solomon, "and even those who are yet to come will not be remembered by those who follow" (Ecclesiastes 1:11).

You are going to die. What a crushing, desperate thought. But unless you swallow hard and embrace it, you are not prepared to live.

Previous generations thought a lot about death. Plague, famine, and war will do that to people. A cough might be the start of something worse; a sunny day might lead to a cloudless week that withers your crops. Even if all goes well, you still have to fight off those who want to steal your stuff. Medieval Christians understood the fragility of this life and the importance of the next, and their leading scholars wrote books entitled *The Art of Dying* and *Preparing for Death*. Unlike today, when people would prefer to die in their sleep or by a blow they never see coming, a medieval person considered a sudden and unexpected end to be the worst possible way to go. Death is too important to sneak up on us. We must be ready for it.

You are going to die.

Many of us are not prepared to die, and for two opposite reasons. First, some of us are so terrified by death that we pull the covers over our heads and try to forget about it. We know everyone dies eventually, yet we pretend it will never happen to us. We're surprised when we are struck by a distracted driver, fall off a roof, or learn that we have cancer. We momentarily sober up when our parents die and we move to the front of the line, but we tell ourselves that new drugs and medical breakthroughs will prolong our lives for several more decades. And so we turn each birthday into a dark joke, with black balloons, over-the-hill cards, and "Happy Birthday" sung in a minor key, hoping good humor will cushion the brutal fact that we are closer to the end of our lives than the beginning.

There is a second, more spiritual obstacle to preparing for death: We don't take it seriously enough. I admire those Christians who have no fear of death. They "desire to depart and be with Christ, which is better by far" (Philippians 1:23), and they honestly wouldn't mind if they died right this minute. But their sense of triumph may have come too easily. Like a fledgling author whose first novel is optioned into a blockbuster movie, or a rookie who leads his football team to a championship on the first try, I'm not sure these giants of the faith can fully appreciate what they've done. It's not easy to write a bestseller or win the Super Bowl, and it's not easy to face death without flinching.

If death was no big deal, then there would be no reason to be a Christian. Every religion purports to solve some significant problem. Buddhism addresses the problem of suffering, which it solves by awakening its followers to the "truth" that suffering, like everything else in the world, is merely an illusion. Hinduism claims that our problem is bad karma, which we can fix by devoting ourselves to every form of deity, including ourselves. Islam says that our problem is pride, which we overcome when we submit to Allah.

> If death was no big deal, then there would be no reason to be a Christian.

And Christianity . . . what problem does our faith solve? Open your Bible in the middle and you'll find people who are wrestling with death. Job sobs that his "days are swifter than a weaver's shuttle, and they come to an end without hope" (7:6). Solomon laments that everyone dies, wise and fool, man and beast alike (Ecclesiastes 2:14–16; 3:18–21).

Their plaintive cry reaches a crescendo in the center of the Psalms, where the writers plead with God to save us from death. "I call to you, O Lord, every day; I spread out my hands to you. Do you show your wonders to the dead? Do those who are dead rise up and praise you?" (88:9–10). Psalm 90 is entirely about death, which Moses blames on sin: "You have set our iniquities before you, our secret sins in the light of your presence. All our days pass away under your wrath . . . their span is but trouble and sorrow, for they quickly pass, and we fly away" (vv. 8–10).

Scripture wrings its hands over death in the middle to set up our great salvation in the end. The New Testament celebrates the good news that God became man "so that by his death he might destroy him who holds the power of death—that is, the devil—and free those who all their lives were held in slavery by their fear of death" (Hebrews 2:14–15).

Sin and death are the one-two punch that Jesus came to knock out. If you think these are nothing to worry about, there is little chance you will give your life to Jesus. If you admit these lethal blows are destroying you, then you probably already know that your only hope lies in Jesus. No other religion even attempts to solve this problem.

Jesus died and rose again to defeat the twin terrors of sin and death. Minimize them—say they are nothing to fear—and you also minimize the sacrifice of Christ that conquers them. Anyone can muddle through minor difficulties, but overcoming sin and death requires an act of God.

> Minimize sin and death—say they are nothing to fear—and you also minimize the sacrifice of Christ that conquers them.

This book will explain what God did and how you may join His victory over death. If you are not yet ready to confront your mortality, you desperately need to read this book. But it is not for you. If you don't care about dying because you are longing for heaven, you could still learn a lot from this book, but it is not meant for you.

This book is for those who understand, maybe for the first time, that they are going to die. Perhaps you received a bleak diagnosis, felt a lump your doctor wants to check out, or maybe you've simply determined to face the one thing more certain than taxes. And you're scared, sickened, and dismayed by the very thought of death.

I promise not to blow sunshine your way. I won't tell you death is not so bad, that it's really just a new form of life or a graduation into glory. I will tell you that death is demonic and degrading, an evil intruder into God's world and "the last enemy" that Jesus will destroy (1 Corinthians 15:26). I will tell you what happens when you die and what you can do about it.

This honest look at death, which occupies the first half of this book, is essential for understanding the hope we have in Jesus. The second half will explore this hope—how Jesus has defeated death and how we may participate in His triumph. If you take what we will learn to heart, you will win the last battle at death and be ready to live today.

Questions for Reflection

1. Do you think too little or too much about death? What worries you most about dying?
2. Is your culture in denial about death? If so, why does this matter? What do we lose when we ignore our inevitable end?
3. Write down the reasons why you want to follow Jesus. How many of these reasons would still be true if Jesus had not defeated death?
4. The devastation of death is intimidating. What does the size of your enemy suggest about the power of its conqueror?

TWO

FOCUS

Teach us to number our days aright, that we
may gain a heart of wisdom.

Psalm 90:12

MATT CHANDLER WAS LIVING LARGE. This thirty-five-year-
old rising pastor had taken all of seven years to lead his Texas
congregation from 160 to 6,000 people on three campuses.
He had the wind at his back until Thanksgiving morning,
when he suddenly suffered a seizure and fell, convulsing in
front of his fireplace and young family. An ambulance rushed
Matt to the hospital, where doctors ran some tests and found
a tumor on the frontal lobe of his brain.

Matt grappled with all of the questions you might expect
for someone in his situation. Was he going to die? Who would
care for his wife and three children? Why him? Why now?

Matt was encouraged by the Christian neurosurgeon who
prepped him for surgery. The doctor told him, "Nothing's
really changed for you—you just get to be aware that you're
mortal. Everybody is, but they're just not aware of it. The
gift that God's given you is that you get to be aware of your
mortality."

In an interview after his surgery, Matt said he had to agree. "So if this goes bad for me, if my MRI scan next month shows that this thing is turning aggressive, then we know that I have a short amount of time, and that lets me talk with my wife, talk with my children. . . . Most guys who die in their thirties kiss their family goodbye in the morning and never come home. . . . In a real sense, there is a real gift I've been given. . . . At least once a year, for the rest of my life, I get to have the anxiety of 'Am I going to hear today that I only have a couple of years to live?' And as difficult as that is in some ways, it really is a gift, to just be aware."

Matt then quoted Ecclesiastes 7:2—"It is better to go to a house of mourning than to go to a house of feasting, for death is the destiny of every man; the living should take this to heart."

> The tentacles of death snake around us, squeezing the air from our lungs and dragging us underwater to the abyss.

It's easy to take death to heart when we've been diagnosed with a brain tumor or ALS or stage four cancer. In such cases we don't take death to heart so much as death takes over our heart, crushing our spirit with gloom and terror. The tentacles of death snake around us, squeezing the air from our lungs and dragging us underwater to the abyss. We understand David's despair: "The waves of death swirled about me; the torrents of destruction overwhelmed me. The cords of the grave coiled around me" (2 Samuel 22:5–6). In desperation we bargain, "O Lord, heal me, for my bones are in agony. . . . Turn, O Lord, and deliver me" for "no one remembers you when he is dead. Who praises you from the grave?" (Psalm 6:2–5). Give me one more chance, God, and I will shout your praises. Let me die and we both lose.

It's more difficult to take death to heart when we don't expect to die soon. But it's not impossible if we remember two things. First, *we could die today*. In a neurotic-sounding section of his *Institutes*, John Calvin lists the many ways we could die: "Embark upon a ship, you are one step away from death. Mount a horse, if one foot slips, your life is imperiled. Go through the city streets, you are subject to as many dangers as there are tiles on the roofs." After warning about weapons, animals, snakes, fire, poison, storms, and robberies gone wrong, Calvin observes that just because such tragedies are rare doesn't mean they won't happen to us.

He's right. Every day we hear of car crashes, homicides, and perfectly healthy people who keel over from heart attacks or strokes. Any of these situations could happen to us. The oncoming car might swerve into our lane, the store might be held up while we're standing in line, and a clot we don't know about could break free and drift to our lung. Unlikely, but these events happen often enough that we should never take our lives for granted.

Second, while the odds are long that we will die today, it is absolutely certain that *this day will die*. Our lives are a series of days that "are swifter than a weaver's shuttle" (Job 7:6), and once they end they never come again. Nothing fritters our lives away faster than living a day or two ahead. We put off what needs to be done, saying we will get around to it tomorrow. Little orphan Annie rightly sings tomorrow is "only a day away." Trouble is, tomorrow is *always* a day away. Tomorrow never comes, and those who live there forget to live here, in the only moment where life actually happens. James reminds us that "you do not even know what will happen tomorrow. What is your life? You are a mist that appears for a little while and then vanishes" (4:14). The sun will soon set on this day, so make something of it before it's gone.

When we take death to heart, we "gain a heart of wisdom" (Psalm 90:12). William Faulkner wrote that "a man can see so much further when he stands in the darkness than he does when, standing in the light, he tries to probe the darkness." So we pray with David, "Show me, O Lord, my life's end and the number of my days; let me know how fleeting is my life" (Psalm 39:4).

As Matt discovered, it really is a gift to know you are going to die. You know the saying, "What doesn't kill you makes you stronger"? It's also true that what kills you makes you stronger, for knowing your life will end focuses your mind on what matters most.

How would your life change if you followed the country-western song and decided to "Live Like You Were Dying"? You might not go skydiving, "Rocky Mountain climbing," or "2.7 seconds on a bull named Fu Manchu," but wouldn't you love deeper, speak sweeter, and give "forgiveness [you'd] been denying"?

Your "bucket list" (things to do before you kick the bucket) might not include such extravagant goals as visiting Stonehenge, seeing the Pyramids, or driving a motorcycle on the Great Wall of China, but it would probably include telling your friends how much you love them, buying what you want rather than what is on sale, and eating more ice cream.

Don't merely be discouraged by death; use it to gain perspective. You will know you have taken death to heart when you stop fretting about the stain on your carpet and the price of gasoline and save your energy for the people and problems that count. You will spend less time online, in the mall, and scrolling through channels on television. You will follow the news and your favorite team with one eye and from a distance, knowing that what happens with the weather or on the field does not change the final score of your life.

You will say no to many things so you can say yes to the best. Life is too short to read bland books or watch movie sequels. There isn't enough time for gossip, grudges, or plotting revenge. You don't have years to waste on what someone else thinks you should be or do. When you take death to heart, you'll tuck your children in every night, make some meals from scratch to share with friends, and go barefoot every chance you can. You'll take hungry bites from the peach of life, and when the juice runs down your chin and all the way to your elbows, you'll wipe it with your shirt.

> Death is the destiny of every person, and those who take that truth to heart are finally ready to live.

Death is the destiny of every person, and those who take that truth to heart are finally ready to live.

Questions for Reflection

1. Read Ecclesiastes 7:2. Why is it "better to go to a house of mourning than to go to a house of feasting"?

2. Have you had a close brush with death? How did the scare change you, and for how long? How might you regularly remind yourself of what you learned then?

3. Skim the obituaries in your local newspaper. How many people died unexpectedly or too young? If they could speak to you now, what do you think they might say?

4. Speak this sentence out loud: "I might die today." How does that truth change the priorities and cares of your day?

THREE

JUDGMENT

Man is destined to die once, and after that to face judgment.

Hebrews 9:27

LAST MONTH A MAN died a mile from my house. Heavy rains from a midnight storm weakened a tree's roots until it fell across the road, and the man's pickup truck slammed into it as he was driving to work in the predawn dark. An orange cone marks the twisted guardrail where his truck ran off the road, and every time I drive past I'm reminded of the fragility of life.

The following week a woman across town was killed while walking with friends. She was startled by a lawn sprinkler that popped out of the ground, and she dodged the spray by stepping off the sidewalk and into the path of a car she never saw. Her death seems especially tragic because it was so avoidable. Who could have imagined that a lawn sprinkler would set off a chain of events that ended in her death?

I did not know either person, but there seems to be an everlasting difference between their two deaths. The woman was a Christian musician from Indonesia who came to town to represent her country in an international conference of churches. Her tragic end was mourned at a memorial service, where her friends testified to her faith in Christ and took comfort that she was now in the presence of her Lord.

I read the man's obituary and stories about his accident, and though his friends said, "He was probably one of the best neighbors you could ever ask for . . . always willing to go the extra mile with anybody," there was sadly no mention that he went to be with his Lord and Savior, or even that he went to church. The obituary simply mentioned his surviving wife and family members and said that the celebration of his life would take place in a clubhouse.

Two people with apparently two destinies. The difference between them is the most important thing you will ever hear, so please read carefully what follows.

The Bible teaches that everyone will live forever in one of two places: either with Jesus on the New Earth or cut off from God in hell (Revelation 20:10–21:4). When something is really bad, we sometimes compare it to hell. We say war is hell, a bad marriage is hell, or a blistering summer day is hot as hell. Not even close. When we talk this way, we show we have no idea how awful hell is.

Scripture uses the most loathsome images to convey the horrors of hell: it's a lake of fire crawling with worms, and the only sounds that pierce the darkness are "weeping and gnashing of teeth" (Revelation 20:10; Mark 9:48; Matthew 8:12). John Calvin noted that Scripture can only use things from our experience to communicate something we've never seen or heard. So as bad as fire, worms, and gnashing teeth seem, the reality of hell is much worse.

Hell is so hellish that some people wonder whether a loving God would really send anyone there. When a friend confided that hell is too horrible to believe, I told him that is precisely the point. Hell is far worse than anything we can imagine, and yet Jesus repeatedly warns us that hell is real. He said it's better to gouge out a lustful eye or cut off a thieving hand than to take both eyes and hands into the lake of fire where the "worm does not die, and the fire is not quenched" (Mark 9:48; see also Matthew 5:29–30).

> Tragically, most people live a mere heartbeat from hell.
>
> ∽∞∽

Tragically, most people live a mere heartbeat from hell. Like a drunk staggering along the mouth of a volcano, oblivious to the fact that he is one slip away from a fiery end, they don't know where they are or even that they're drunk. Most drunks think they're fine. They are insulted when a police officer pulls them over, and they proudly use the opportunity to slur the alphabet and tipsily walk a jagged line. They are genuinely surprised and even a bit angry when the unimpressed officer cuffs and hauls them to jail. Likewise most people—drunk on their own excellence—honestly believe they are too good to go to hell. Hell is for evil people, not nice folks like them.

This belief in their own goodness has changed the way most people think about death. Previous generations feared death because they were afraid of going to hell. Almost no one fears hell anymore. The dying may suffer existential angst—they fear falling out of existence into an infinite void of emptiness—but they don't think they are candidates for hell. This is why most people are more nervous about the process of dying than death itself. "I'm not afraid to die," they say. "I'm only afraid of getting dead."

This statement is disastrously naive, for Scripture teaches that we are sinners, born guilty and corrupted with Adam's sin (Romans 3:9–20; 5:12–21). This is an offensive belief to some, but every parent knows it's true. We didn't teach our children to scratch and scream—they came that way. We all want to play God, to do what we want when and how we want, and we don't want anyone, even and especially God, to cramp our style.

Our attempts to play God pull us from God, who is life, and so we eventually die. Then we face the music, for "we must all appear before the judgment seat of Christ, that each one may receive what is due him for the things done while in the body, whether good or bad" (2 Corinthians 5:10). If you think about it, none of us could ever do enough good to offset even one sin against our holy God. Any good that we might do is already owed Him, so how could we possibly do surplus good works to pay back our debt? Left to ourselves, we would all go to hell, the fitting penalty for trying to overthrow the reign of God in our lives.

But the best news you'll ever hear is that God has not left us to stumble our way into hell. His Son lived without sin, submitting to God where we did not, and then He offered His perfect life in our place on the cross. If we confess our sin and put our faith in Christ—trusting Him alone for our salvation—then God our Father credits Jesus' good life to us and receives us as righteous on account of His Son (Romans 3:22–26). Jesus went to hell so we don't have to.

> Jesus went to hell so we don't have to.
>
> ⌒⌒⌒

If you have never repented of your sin and trusted Jesus for your right standing with God, why don't you do so now? Tell God that you are sorry for living by your own rules and that you want to find your life in Him. If you're not sure what to say, you could start with this simple prayer: "Heavenly Father, I know I am a sinner and that my sin is killing me now and will send me to hell forever. I turn my back on my sin and put my faith in your dear Son.

I believe Jesus died on the cross in my place and arose from the dead to defeat sin, death, and Satan. Please count me righteous for Jesus' sake, and send your Spirit to empower me to please you with a life of gratitude. Amen."

If you have entrusted yourself to Jesus, be sure to join a church so you can grow in your salvation and encourage others in the body of Christ. You belong to the family of God, and you will live forever with Jesus when He returns to restore our world. All of the promises and counsel in the rest of this book are for you.

If you have not turned from your sin to Jesus, then sadly none of the gospel promises in the following chapters apply to you. You are literally playing with fire. I beg you to meditate on these words from Hebrews: "Man is destined to die once, and after that to face judgment." "It is a dreadful thing to fall into the hands of the living God," for "God is a consuming fire." "But we see Jesus . . . now crowned with glory and honor because he suffered death, so that by the grace of God he might taste death for everyone" (9:27; 10:31; 12:29; 2:9).

Have you given your life to Jesus? Then turn the page. The next chapter is for you.

Questions for Reflection

1. Do you believe that hell is real? How does this belief change the way you live?

2. Do you think you deserve to go to hell?

3. What does the cross indicate about what we deserve? Would Jesus have died on the cross if we weren't in danger of going to hell?

4. What are you counting on to avoid hell: your own goodness, the sacrifice of Jesus, or something else?

FOUR

FEAR

By his death he might . . . free those who all
their lives were held in slavery by their fear of
death.

Hebrews 2:14–15

WHICH OF THESE MEN died well? One man was wrongly
convicted and sentenced to drink a cup of poison. He cheer-
fully took the cup from the executioner, raised it to the heavens, and prayed for a happy life beyond the grave. Then he
swallowed the poison and lay down to die. When his friends
began to weep, he chided them: "You are strange fellows;
what is wrong with you? I sent the women away for this very
purpose, to stop their creating such a scene. I have heard that
one should die in silence. So please be quiet and keep control
of yourselves."

The other man was also unjustly convicted and con-
demned to die. But rather than calmly accept His fate, He
agonized over what lay ahead. He prayed, "Father, if you are
willing, take this cup from me" (Luke 22:42), and He cried
out in the moment of death, "My God, my God, why have you
forsaken me?" (Matthew 27:46).

If we didn't know the second man was Jesus, we might be tempted to think that the first man is a better model for how we should die. And in fact, that is why Plato gave us this story of Socrates's death. He wanted everyone to follow the example of his wise teacher and calmly embrace death as the entrance into the next, happy life. Sadly, Socrates was not a follower of the true God, and his stoic acceptance of death was tragically out of step with the hell that awaited him.

But what are we to make of Jesus' anguish in the face of death? For starters, we should note that His was not just any death. Jesus did not shrink from the pain of physical death—as excruciating as His crucifixion was—but He cried out from the hell of being rejected by His Father. That unbearable moment seems impossible, for the Father lives in the Son and the Son lives in the Father (John 17:21), yet somehow the triune God was torn apart as the perfect Son of God became sin for us (2 Corinthians 5:21).

Neither should we criticize Jesus for dying with less dignity than us, for the only reason we can die in peace is because Jesus has gone before us and broken the trail. Jesus has done all of the heavy lifting. We can rest in His salvation, knowing we will never be forsaken by God because Jesus was.

Jesus' death was more painful and profound than anything we can experience, and yet His example does prove that fear is not the opposite of faith. The same Son who cringed, "take this cup from me," also said, "yet not my will, but yours be done" (Luke 22:42). Shortly after despairing, "Why have you forsaken me?" (Matthew 27:46; Mark 15:34), Jesus reaffirmed His faith, "Father, into your hands I commit my spirit" (Luke 23:46).

Faith means to trust, rely, or commit. We act in faith when we put all of our weight on the promises of God, regardless of how confident we feel. Last summer I rode a zip line for the first time, which was quite an accomplishment for me because I'm terrified of heights. I did not feel very safe as I shuffled off the forty-foot-high platform, but my wobbly faith was enough. I trusted my life to that slender cable as much as my brave friends, who laughed and waved as they jumped off backward. Faith doesn't require good form; it only requires that we go all in.

> Fear is not the opposite of faith, for fear presents an opportunity for faith.

Fear is not the opposite of faith, for fear presents an opportunity for faith. As Peter and the disciples learned when Jesus approached their storm-tossed boat, anyone can walk on land, but only true believers lower themselves over the boat's edge and slosh toward Jesus (Matthew 14:22–33). Faith does not ignore our fear of death and pretend that everything is okay. But with shaky knees and sweaty palms, faith swallows hard and clings to God's promise that we will live again. Death is "the king of terrors" (Job 18:14), and for that reason it provides the ultimate test of our faith.

Hebrews 2:15 says Jesus' death frees "those who all their lives were held in *slavery* by their fear of death" (emphasis added). Notice the text does not say we are freed from all *fear* of death. There are days and moods when I worry about dying. Augustine understood. He told his church, "Those who do not fear death should examine themselves closely lest perhaps they are in fact already dead."

Death raises many fears. Some are troubled by what will happen to their body after they're gone, while others fear for the loved ones they leave behind. Some people fear the process of dying. Will they lose their dignity and ability to manage the pain? Many are afraid of the great beyond. Who really knows what happens when we die? As Shakespeare said in *Hamlet*,

To die: to sleep.
To sleep? Perchance to dream. Ay, there's
 the rub;
For in that sleep of death what dreams may
 come. . . .
The undiscovered country from whose
 bourn
No traveler returns, puzzles the will,
And makes us rather bear those ills we have
Than fly to others that we know not of.

We are not guaranteed freedom from all fear of death, much like a school cafeteria is not guaranteed to be free of peanuts. An alert lunchroom monitor will catch most offenders, but there will always be a contraband Snickers or chunky peanut butter and jelly sandwich that clever students smuggle into school. Likewise, we will be less troubled by death when we understand how Jesus has defeated it, but that won't stop a stray fear from popping up every now and again.

Jesus has not eliminated all fear of death, but he has freed us from the *slavery* of the fear of death. We may have moments when we feel afraid, but we are no longer paralyzed by our fears. Subsequent chapters will explore how Jesus has broken the bondage of death; for now, here are two keys for keeping faith in the middle of your fears.

> You will keep faith as long as you trust God to remain faithful after you die.

First, you will keep faith as long as you trust God to remain faithful after you die. Take a moment to reflect on your life. Consider the many ways God has blessed you and your family. Is it likely that the God who has been good to you here and now will not continue to be faithful in the life to come? Paul argues that the God who sacrificed His only Son can be trusted to remain faithful forever:

> He who did not spare his own Son, but gave him up for us all—how will he not also, along with him, graciously give us all things? . . . For I am convinced that neither *death* nor life, neither angels nor demons, neither the present nor the future, nor any powers, neither height nor depth, nor anything else in all creation, will be able to separate us from the love of God that is in Christ Jesus our Lord. (Romans 8:32, 38–39; emphasis added)

God is committed to you. He overcame enormous odds just to conceive you—you would not exist if just one parent were changed in your family tree. He brought you into this world and sustains you, providing for all your needs and many of your wants. He gave His life for you and even now is preparing you to conquer death and reign with Him in the life to come. God hasn't invested so much to turn back now. You can trust Him to remain faithful even after you're dead. It will be true for you as it was with Abraham, Isaac, and Jacob. Although these patriarchs no longer walk the earth, Jesus claimed they are still alive in God's presence. God remains their God, and "he is not the God of the dead, but of the living, for to him all are alive" (Luke 20:38).

Second, you will keep faith when you recognize that God is with you in your moment of death. We tend to think we die alone. Our friends and family may walk us to the brink of death, but we must take the last step by ourselves. That is not entirely true. Paul explains, "Christ died and returned to life so that he might be the Lord of both the dead and the living."

So "whether we live or die, we belong to the Lord" (Romans 14:8–9).

You do not die alone, but with your Lord who went before and now walks you through the valley of the shadow of death. You will never endure anything Jesus has not already suffered. You will never endure anything He is not right now suffering with you.

Death is scary, but you have a hand to hold. It bears the scars from a previous death, and it's holding you.

Questions for Reflection

1. Why does Job 18:14 call death "the king of terrors"?

2. What questions or doubts do you have about the after-life? Where can you turn for answers?

3. Write a letter to God thanking him for all the ways He has been faithful to you throughout your life. Then tell Him you're counting on Him to remain faithful after you die.

4. Read Romans 8:32–39 and list all of the enemies that cannot separate you from God. What does this mean for you?

FIVE

ANGER

In the prime of my life must I go through the gates of death and be robbed of the rest of my years?

Isaiah 38:10

IF ISRAEL HAD A Mount Rushmore, King Hezekiah would be on it. Hezekiah had the heart of David and the wealth of Solomon, and he used his success to rout the Philistines and thumb his nose at the mighty Assyrians. "I'm in charge now," he told their king, "and we will no longer bow to your impotent idols or pay you tribute. So scram!"

About that time Hezekiah became seriously ill, and the prophet Isaiah told him to put his house in order, for God said he was going to die. There is never a good time to die, but the timing here was especially bad. Hezekiah was in his late thirties and had no children. If he died without producing an heir, the line of David would end with him, a sure sign he had been cursed by God.

But why? Hezekiah had done everything right. He had smashed the idols in Judah and restored the temple and its worship of the true God. He was God's man in God's place at

God's time. He was the only reason the godless Assyrians had not turned Judah into a smoldering pile of rubble.

Hezekiah would not accept this end to his life, and he reminded God that he deserved better. He prayed, "Remember, O Lord, how I have walked before you faithfully and with wholehearted devotion and have done what is good in your eyes." Am I really going to die "in the prime of my life . . . robbed of the rest of my years?" Hezekiah could not stand the injustice, and he "wept bitterly" (Isaiah 38:3, 10).

I can relate. If I knew I was going to die soon, I would probably become angry with God. This is how you treat the people who love you? I have a family that needs me. Why don't you take someone who doesn't contribute? How come the obese chain smoker who wastes her welfare check at the casino and her evenings watching reality television is doing okay and I am going to die? This isn't fair!

Anger is our response to some perceived slight or injustice. We become angry when we feel we have been mistreated or given less than we deserve. So the anger we feel when we are dying raises the question: What do we deserve from God?

At first glance, it seems we have every right to expect God to take care of us. After all, we did not ask to be here. We had no say in whether we would be conceived and born. God and our parents took care of that, and here we are. At the very least, we expect the God who brought us into existence to keep us alive.

God himself declares that He is our Father, eager "to give good gifts to those who ask him!" (Matthew 7:11). Jesus says we should not worry about the daily necessities of life, for "your heavenly Father knows that you need them." If you "seek first his kingdom and his righteousness," then "all these things will be given to you as well" (Matthew 6:31–33). Isn't this an open-ended promise to provide for our needs? Don't we who are dying have the right to ask why God hasn't kept His Word?

It seems so. God volunteered the promise of protection, and we should tell Him when the bread we asked for tastes like a stone or the fish we wanted looks like a snake (Matthew 7:9–10). He has broad shoulders, and He can take it. Remember that Job vented about God for twenty chapters, and when God finally appeared He was more pleased with Job's angry charge of injustice than with his three friends' pious defense of God's honor (Job 42:8). Besides, God already knows when we're angry with Him, so we might as well tell Him.

Fair enough. But justice in our situation is complicated, for we have compromised our rights by our complicity in Adam's sin. We may not have eaten the forbidden fruit, but our DNA was present in Adam and we daily side with his doomed attempt to overthrow God's authority in our lives. We want to play God, and the penalty for that is death (Genesis 3:19).

Adam and Eve deserved to die the moment they sinned against God. The entire world should have dissolved like cotton candy on the tongue. You and I, who are guilty of Adam's sin, should never have been born.

Viewed from this angle, it is apparent that God has graciously given us far more than we deserve. My mentor used to say every time something did not go his way, "Oh well, I deserve hell, so this little problem is a bonus!" He did not despair over his lifelong battle with chronic fatigue syndrome, but considered that even his half-days of stamina were better than the swift death he deserved.

If you knew you were going to die today, you would rightly grieve over lost opportunities—the child you did not see grow up, the trip you never took, or the assignment you never finished. You may even cry out like Hezekiah, "Is this how you treat those who love you?" But you also should count what you have gained—the people you have loved, the places you have lived, and the projects you have completed, and remember that each of these is an undeserved gift of God.

God has not promised to keep us alive indefinitely. Unless Jesus returns, everyone will eventually die of something. The immediate cause may be an accident, a virus, or just old age, but the ultimate cause is always sin. So if you're going to be angry at something, get mad at sin—and at yourself for doing it. The truth is if we weren't sinners, we wouldn't die.

> If we weren't sinners, we wouldn't die.

Still, just because we are going to die someday doesn't mean we have to die now, and if we look around it is easy to find lesser people who have it better than us. This is Asaph's complaint in Psalm 73, for he "envied . . . the prosperity of the wicked," who seem to "have no struggles" and "are free from the burdens common to man" (vv. 3–5). Asaph pulled out of his funk when he took the long view. He realized that though the wicked are carefree and wealthy now, their lives will end in ruin (vv. 12, 18–20).

> You may be dying with nothing but God, but that is enough.

In a few years we will all be dead. What then? Asaph concluded the only thing he really wanted out of life was to know and love God, who is life itself. "Whom have I in heaven but you?" he prayed. "And earth has nothing I desire besides you. My flesh and my heart may fail, but God is the strength of my heart and my portion forever" (vv. 25–26).

You may not have it as nice as other people. You may not have caught their breaks, received their promotions, or raised their honor roll kids.

You may be dying way too soon, with too little to put in your obituary. You may be dying with nothing but God, but that is enough.

Memorize Asaph's prayer and claim it as your own: "I am always with you; you hold me by my right hand. You guide me with your counsel, and afterward you will take me into glory" (vv. 23–24).

Really, what more could you want out of life?

Questions for Reflection

1. Think of someone who has treated you unfairly. How does God want you to respond?

2. Do you believe that God has been unfair to you? Do you think that God would agree?

3. What should you do when you think that God is not giving what you deserve?

4. An old chorus states that "Christ is all I need." How have you found this to be true in your life?

SIX

SORROW

Jesus wept.

John 11:35

CHRISTOPHER HITCHENS WAS DYING. An outspoken athe-ist, Hitchens somberly explained that years of smoking and drinking had left him with cancer of the esophagus. He tried to be brave, telling the interviewer that his cancer had not tempted him to call out to God, and any desperate prayers he might yet offer would prove only that he was no longer in his right mind. But his weary eyes and thinning sprigs of hair exposed a beaten man who was dreading the few torturous months he had left.

The interview was especially sad because of Hitchens's belief that he was losing everything. He assumed that when he died, his life would fade to black, dissolving into an eternity of nothingness. He might encourage himself that being dead is no different than being unborn, that just as he did not mind not existing before his birth, so he won't be troubled by not existing after his death. But the difference is that now he has everything to lose—every thought he has ever had and every pleasure he has ever enjoyed will perish with him. He will never pass this way again, and so he will try anything, even the toxins of chemotherapy, to prolong his life for one more day.

Even sadder is that Hitchens is wrong about what will happen when he dies. He will not slip into nothingness, but in a terrible surprise too horrible to contemplate, he will escape the burning pain of chemotherapy only to wake up in hell. Hitchens's stiff upper lip in the face of his demise is tragically inadequate, but it is all anyone can do who does not know God.

Christians approach death from a much better place. Like Hitchens, John Calvin's death was largely self-inflicted. He worked relentlessly on one meal a day, and his body gave out by the time he was fifty-six. Calvin suffered most of his life from migraines, kidney stones, and coughing spells that became so violent that they burst blood vessels in his lungs. Yet he continued to drive his body. When he could not walk to church to deliver his sermon, he was carried on a chair. When he was too weak to leave his room, his students would crowd into his bedroom to hear his lectures. When urged to rest, he responded, "What! Would you have the Lord find me idle when he comes?"

Perhaps because his body had long betrayed him, Calvin didn't seem to miss a beat when he passed from this life to the next. He called his fellow ministers into his room, and recounting how God had used him to reform the church, assured them that God would continue the work long after he was gone. Calvin did not weep for his loss, in part because he wasn't wired that way and in part because he didn't see death as a loss. Death was his ticket to heaven. How could he be sad?

While I appreciate Calvin's heavenly perspective, his approach to death can be a Christian form of denial. Paul declares that Christians should not "grieve like the rest of men, who have no hope" (1 Thessalonians 4:13). Paul does not say Christians should not grieve—he expects that we will—only that we should not grieve like those who do not know God.

Christopher Hitchens grieves because his life is a total loss, even worse than he knows. He believes he has no future, so all he can do is sink his fingernails into the present and try to hang on for one more miserable day.

Christians are delivered from this despair that comes with total loss, but we still lose a lot when we die. Consider the loved ones we leave behind and the plans we leave undone. If we learn that we will die young, we grieve that we never married or started our careers. The world will never know what it lost in our passing. If we are about to die in our forties, we grieve that we didn't live long enough to launch our children, hold our grandchildren, or complete some project we began years ago. If we live to old age, we may weep even more when we approach death, for now we know precisely what we are giving up. We're not merely losing potential spouses and children, but we're saying goodbye to people we have loved for half a century or more.

> It wouldn't be human to feel this coming loss and not weep. Nor divine.

It wouldn't be human to feel this coming loss and not weep. Nor divine. The smallest verse in the Bible is also the most comforting: "Jesus wept" (John 11:35). Imagine the implications. The Son of God was "deeply moved in spirit and troubled" at Lazarus's tomb (v. 33). Even though He knew He was going to make everything better by raising Lazarus from the dead, Jesus took time to mourn with those who were devastated by their loss.

He still does. Jesus loves you as He loved Lazarus, and He weeps with you as He wept for Lazarus. Jesus feels every sorrow you suffer, only more. He hurts when you hurt because "he cares for you" (1 Peter 5:7), and He has an infinite capacity to sympathize because He is God. Jesus is our "great high priest" who can "sympathize with our weaknesses," for He "has been tempted in every way, just as we are—yet was without sin" (Hebrews 4:14–15).

When we pour out our troubles to Jesus, we bare our souls to a God who gets it. There is no suffering we can ever experience that He has not already endured. Abandoned by friends? His disciples "deserted him and fled" (Mark 14:50). Feeling forsaken by God? He actually was. Dreading death? He sweat blood. Because we have such a compassionate Savior, we should "approach the throne of grace with confidence, so that we may receive mercy and find grace to help us in our time of need" (Hebrews 4:16).

Jesus wept. He did not use the concept of Romans 8:28 as a club, telling Mary and Martha, "All things work together for good so you should really look for the silver lining here. It's actually a good thing your brother is dead." He didn't treat their loss as anything other than what it was—a loss that triggered the tears of God.

But Jesus did not weep as those who have no hope. He told Martha, "I am the resurrection and the life. He who believes in me will live, even though he dies; and whoever lives and believes in me will never die. Do you believe this?" (John 11:25–26).

Do you believe this? It changes everything if you do. Your hope in the resurrection will not eliminate your present grief, but it will give you patience to endure it. You won't drown in the despair of those who die without God, for you know that the same Jesus who called, "Lazarus, come out!" will someday descend from heaven and shout the same command into your grave (John 11:43; 1 Thessalonians 4:16).

You may shiver as you walk through the shadow of death, but the shadow itself is cast by the bright light of the resurrection. "Weeping may remain for a night, but rejoicing comes in the morning" (Psalm 30:5). One morning you will rise, and every tear will be wiped from your eyes (Revelation 21:4). So go ahead and weep, but only as someone who knows how your story ends. It doesn't.

> You may shiver as you walk through the shadow of death, but the shadow itself is cast by the bright light of the resurrection.

Questions for Reflection

1. Have you grieved over your approaching death?

2. Do you believe that Jesus grieves with you, as He wept at Lazarus's tomb (John 11:35)?

3. Write your own psalm of lament. See Psalm 102 for inspiration.

4. Meditate on Psalm 116:15, "Precious in the sight of the Lord is the death of his saints." How does this help you in your grief?

SEVEN

REGRET

Godly sorrow brings repentance that leads to salvation and leaves no regret, but worldly sorrow brings death.

2 Corinthians 7:10

MY GRANDFATHER WAS SAVED at a rescue mission. He had relied on liquor to numb the pain of being poor, which only inflicted more misery upon his long-suffering wife and dozen children. This vicious cycle of pain, alcohol, and more hurt finally ended when he found his salvation in Christ. When my mother went to the mission to see her father, she could tell by the sound of his footsteps coming down the hall that he was a changed man. Jesus not only saved his soul, but also He graciously removed any desire for alcohol. Grandpa never drank again.

Near the end of his life, Grandpa asked the director of the mission to visit him. He had been thinking about the early years when he abandoned his family for the local bar, and he wondered whether God had fully forgiven him. Shouldn't God make him pay for the many evenings he wasn't there for his wife and kids?

My grandfather's story is not unusual. Many people grow old with deep, self-inflicted wounds. Some people are bothered by the years they wasted. They wonder if they stayed too long in that career, with that company, while others wonder if they gave it enough time. If they had stuck it out a bit longer, perhaps their luck would have changed.

Some regret that they didn't play to win. What if they had the courage to take their shot—to go after the date who seemed out of their league, to apply for the job that seemed two rungs too high, or to buy in when everyone else was selling? Others wish they had played it safe. They took one too many risks—with the job or stock market—and they lost their shirt. If they could have a do-over, they would enjoy the modest comforts they had and not fret about what they didn't.

Even worse than the regret of waste is the sorrow of hurting the ones you love. It's one thing to let opportunities slip through your fingers; it's another to be the offender. Many people live with the regret of knowing they broke their wedding vows and bailed on their spouse. Others were absent and angry parents who frittered away their child-rearing years buried in work or blowing up at their charges. Some have committed crimes so unspeakably heinous there is no way they can ever make it right. What hope do they have as they prepare to meet their Maker?

> No one reaches the end of life without some regret.

To rise above regret, we must first recognize that it's inevitable. Despite our pledge to "live like we are dying," no one reaches the end of life without some regret. We wish we had played more, splurged more, and written more love notes to our family and friends. We wish we had worried less, fought less, and watched less television. That's life in a fallen world.

Sinners like us aren't going to avoid all regret, but we can learn to grow through it. We must accept the fact that the only perfect person is Jesus Christ. Jesus is the only person who could honestly say He completed the work He was sent here to do (John 17:4). He left earth with no regret, for He obeyed God fully as He brought salvation to the world.

Nothing you do will ever come close. You may wish you had done more with your life, perhaps cured a disease, built an invention, or led a country or corporation. You regret your name will not be memorized by future schoolchildren and your home will not be turned into a museum. So what? All of these accomplishments are short-lived. Nations and businesses eventually fail, technology grows stale, and new viruses arise to be fought. If you are going to find true and lasting success, you're going to have to find yourself in Jesus.

This is Paul's point when he said, "Whatever was to my profit I now consider loss for the sake of Christ. What is more, I consider everything a loss compared to the surpassing greatness of knowing Christ Jesus my Lord, for whose sake I have lost all things. I consider them rubbish, that I may gain Christ" (Philippians 3:7–8).

How do we find ourselves in Jesus? Paul tells us, "I have been crucified with Christ and I no longer live, but Christ lives in me. The life I live in the body, I live *by faith* in the Son of God, who loved me and gave himself for me" (Galatians 2:20, emphasis added).

Faith is the mechanism that unites us to Jesus. When we put our trust in Jesus, we jump across two thousand years of history to identify with Him. Our years of waste and sin are replaced with His perfect life, which now counts for us. "Therefore," Paul writes, "if anyone is in Christ, he is a new creation; the old has gone, the new has come!" (2 Corinthians 5:17).

Faith in Christ is the only way to get to the other side of regret. Paul writes that "worldly sorrow brings death," for it is unable to do anything to fix our problem (2 Corinthians 7:10). We may feel sorry about our life of sin, but what can we do about it? Nothing but wait for death, when we must face the music for our wasted lives.

But "godly sorrow brings repentance that leads to salvation and leaves no regret" (v. 10). Rather than beat ourselves up for our sin, we must stop thinking about ourselves and grab hold of Jesus. When Satan accuses us—"How can you live with yourself after what you have done?"—we simply agree with him. "You are right," we reply, "and we are far worse than you say. But we are hiding in Jesus, and His righteousness counts for us. If you have anything further to say, we suggest you take it up with Him." When we use every wince of regret as an excuse to run to Jesus, we turn what would normally destroy us into an opportunity to celebrate our salvation.

> When we use every wince of regret as an excuse to run to Jesus, we turn what would normally destroy us into an opportunity to celebrate our salvation.

Such faith may be hard to come by, so God has not left us to ourselves. Previous generations prepared for death by confessing their sin to a priest and receiving his promise of forgiveness. While we do not need to go through a priest to get to God, we will benefit when we confess our sin to a pastor who assures us that we are forgiven. This is why my grandfather called for his spiritual mentor. He *read* in the Bible that his sins were forgiven, but he could not die in peace until he *heard* the words, "God knows your past, and He forgives all of it. You may fall asleep in His cradle of grace."

If we have received Jesus' forgiveness and been reconciled to God, we must also attempt to reconcile with others. This is one of the hardest tasks we will ever do, for we have to swallow a lot of pride to ask others to forgive us. We immediately think of plausible reasons not to—what we did was no big deal, they probably don't even remember, or perhaps they were partly at fault—but deep down we know these are just excuses.

Those who are dying often report a strong urge to settle their accounts with others. Even in the rare cases where forgiveness is not granted, they still die with a clear conscience because they did everything in their power to leave this world with no loose ends.

You may feel nervous and a bit embarrassed to talk to some people. If your sin was especially damaging, you might want to send a letter or use an intermediary to make the first contact. But do reach out. Pray for courage and pick up the phone. It is one act you will never regret.

Questions for Reflection

1. What is your largest regret? Do you need to ask someone for forgiveness?

2. Do you believe that Jesus can release you from the guilt of your worst sin? Why is it a sin to think that he can't?

3. Have you received God's forgiveness for your sins? If so, how would you describe the feeling of knowing that you are forgiven?

4. Are you troubled by memories of what you have done? What should you do when these thoughts pop into your mind?

EIGHT

SIN

Sin entered the world through one man, and death through sin, and in this way death came to all men, because all sinned.

Romans 5:12

IN HIS BESTSELLING BOOK *Tuesdays with Morrie,* Mitch Albom describes the agonizingly slow-motion death of his mentor. Morrie Schwartz was dying in pieces. A.L.S. methodically inched up his body, melting the nerves in his legs and torso until it finally shut down the muscles in his arms and head. In one of their last conversations, Morrie explained why, although he didn't necessarily believe in God, he wasn't afraid to die.

"Death is as natural as life," Morrie said. "The fact that we make such a big hullabaloo over it is all because we don't see ourselves as part of nature. We think because we're human we're something above nature. We're not. Everything that gets born, dies."

Morrie's shrug of resignation is the best our world can offer. Read any book or serious reflection on death and you're almost certain to find these words: *Death is a natural part of life.*

It isn't good or bad, it's just the way life is. Death is normal, a necessary step in the circle of life. We need to pass on to make room for the younger generation. Consider the logjam if no one ever died!

This standard line is intended to comfort those who are dying, but how much does it really help? Imagine coming home to find that someone has stolen all of your belongings and set your house on fire. You frantically call 9-1-1 only to hear the dispatcher respond, "Calm down. We've been getting a lot of these calls lately. Burglary and arson are the new normal."

"Normal?!" you shout into the phone. "I don't care how normal you think they are! Send the police and fire department! Do something!"

Or imagine you're cruising over the Pacific Ocean when the pilot's voice comes over the loudspeaker. "Folks, it looks like our engines have failed, which to be honest, is not surprising for this make and model. It's typical for them to give out after 150,000 miles, but, hey, they had a nice run. Brace yourselves for impact, and remember, we're not the first plane to crash. It's more common than you think."

This reminder is about as helpful as Gautama the Buddha's, who comforted his disciple by saying, "Do not cry, dear Ananda. I have always taught that death is a natural part of life. It is nothing to fear. You must understand that. And when I am gone, let my teachings be your guide. If you have understood them in your heart, you have no more need of me."

Notice that the Buddha has no answer for the problem of death. All he can say is it's really not that bad, because everyone does it. But I don't see the connection. What if death is something really bad that happens to everyone?

The worst part about this death-is-normal view is that it leaves us in despair. If death is a natural part of life, then nothing can be done about it. If it's natural, then nothing *ought* to be done about it. All that's left is to make the best of a situation that is much worse than we're willing to admit.

Morrie told Mitch Albom that death is not so bad because the dead continue to live in our memory. "As long as we can love each other, and remember the feeling of love we had, we can die without ever really going away. All the love you created is still there. All the memories are still there. You live on—in the hearts of everyone you have touched and nurtured while you were here. . . . Death ends a life, not a relationship."

Even if it were enough to be nothing more than someone's memory, this form of existence won't last longer than a generation or two. When was the last time you thought about your great-grandparents? In two generations that will be you—out of sight, out of mind, out of existence.

Yoda thought he was doing better when he told Anakin, "Death is a natural part of life. Rejoice for those around you who transform into the Force." What Yoda failed to mention is that the divine Force is an impersonal power, so you can only join when you as a person slough away. Yoda's Eastern pantheism sounds like a compliment—you are God!—but it turns out that you are actually the problem. Whatever makes you a unique individual has to burn off so the impersonal force buried within can drop and dissipate into the ocean of deity.

The atheist Richard Dawkins takes a more honest approach. He concedes he won't survive his own death, but he consoles himself that "being dead will be no different from being unborn—I shall be just as I was in the time of William the Conqueror or the dinosaurs or the trilobites." Besides being dreadfully mistaken, Dawkins's belief is unsatisfying on its own merits (who wants to go out of existence?). But it's the best his view can hope for—cross your fingers and pray everything fades to black.

The Christian faith offers a better way. Scripture teaches that our death is an unnatural intruder into God's world, a result of Adam's sin that ruined us and every good thing God made. We and our world are now abnormal, so bent and twisted by sin that we eventually die. Death happens to everyone, but this does not mean we were meant to die.

> Death happens to everyone, but this does not mean we were meant to die.

Consider a father who passes a defective gene for lung cancer on to his children, each of which compounds the problem by smoking a pack of cigarettes a day. No doctor would throw up his hands and conclude lung cancer is simply natural for this family. Rather he will devise a plan, such as gene therapy, to repair their broken nature and strongly recommend they not make their condition worse by smoking.

Likewise, Scripture declares that Adam's sin corrupted his nature, which he passed on to us. We ratify our sinful nature by smoking packs of sin each day, and so we die both for Adam's sin and our own. Despite what death certificates often say, no one has ever died of purely natural causes.

> No one has ever died of purely natural causes.

This honest and harsh assessment offers hope. It's encouraging to know death is a problem, for we don't look for solutions to problems that don't exist. When my wife took our crying baby to see the doctor, she was always relieved when he found something wrong. She didn't want to hear that it's normal for children to wail uncontrollably while pulling on their ears, and in a few months they usually outgrow it. If our child is sick, we can hope for a cure, and if nature is broken, we can hope for a fix.

It's good news to know we have a problem, and it's even better news to learn the source of the problem is us. We may not want to admit we are the problem, but consider the alternative. In T. S. Eliot's play *The Cocktail Party*, Celia says, "I should really *like* to think there's something wrong with me—Because, if there isn't, then there's something wrong . . . with the world itself—and that's much more frightening!"

If death was simply the way of the world, there would be nothing anyone could do about it. We would all be victims along for the ride. But if death is unnatural, if it is the horrible end of our sinful rebellion against God, there's hope for that.

Questions for Reflection

1. Why is it a relief to know that death isn't a normal, natural part of life?

2. Do you want people to remember you a hundred years after you die? Why or why not? Does recognition after death matter?

3. Richard Dawkins wrote, "Being dead will be no different from being unborn." Besides being dangerously wrong, why is this view deeply unsatisfying?

4. If death is caused by sin, then how should you think about sin? What should you feel toward books, movies, and websites that glorify sin?

NINE

GUILT

Everyone has turned away, they have together become corrupt; there is no one who does good, not even one.

Psalm 53:3

WHAT DO YOU DO when a dying patient with a low quality of life goes into cardiac arrest? Doctors don't want to cause discomfort by inserting a breathing tube, shocking the heart with a defibrillator, or cracking ribs through chest compressions, so they sometimes go through the motions of resuscitation without really trying to revive the patient. They call this procedure "slow code" or "show code," for it is performed merely for the sake of the family that wants "everything to be done."

One doctor confessed that the "show code" wouldn't be necessary if physicians and their patients were able to have frank conversations about death. "We live in a culture that is in a profound state of denial that death is a natural part of life," she said. "And as a result of that, physicians who are merely products of that culture have tremendous difficulty communicating about care of the end-of-life."

The doctor is right that our culture is in denial about the inevitability of death, but her claim that death is natural shows that she too is in denial. Although her daily work immerses her in the evidence of pain and suffering, she seems unaware that we live in a broken world where death is God's punishment for sin. In her view, we haven't done anything to deserve death; it's just the way life is.

There is another reason we think we don't deserve to die. Everyone agrees death is about the worst thing that can happen to a person, which is why we describe bad situations with the metaphor of death. When we are embarrassed, we say, "I was so humiliated I nearly died." When we experience intense suffering, we say the pain was worse than death. And when our team is losing badly, we say our side is getting killed. Death is Grade A trouble—it turns anger into murder, legal penalties into *capital* punishment, and racism into "the *final* solution" of genocide.

If death is such a terrible evil, we'd like to think that few people could be bad enough to deserve it. And if most of us don't deserve to die, the only option left is to say that death is somehow a natural part of life. But what if the unthinkable is true and we actually deserve death? Then the horror of death would provide a window into our ugly hearts. If we deserve to die, how wicked must we be?

Look at this from God's perspective. If desperate situations call for extreme measures, then extreme measures are a sign we are in a desperate situation. When a police car flashes its lights behind me, my wife may say in her disapproving voice, "What did you do?" If my car is surrounded by a convoy of police cars and a television helicopter is hovering overhead, my wife's tone becomes more accusatory, "*What* did you *do*?" If a fighter jet joins the chase, dropping bombs in the direction of our car, my wife may scream like the leading lady in an action movie, "What did you do?!"

Consider what God did to save us. He didn't hand us a brochure, as if our problem was merely ignorance. He didn't hold an intervention, as if our problem was merely stubbornness. He answered our need with the cross, which can only mean we have royally messed up. If the cross is necessary to save us, then *what did we do?*

We have rebelled against God, causing both our death and Jesus'. We are not victims, but cold-blooded killers whose mutiny has brought death upon ourselves and the Son of God who rescues us. We stand in sinful solidarity with the Jews who shouted to Pilate, "Let his blood be on us and on our children!" (Matthew 27:25). We do not merely cower before the monster of death, but we *are* the moral monster who preys upon ourselves, others, and God. "The sting of death is sin," writes Paul (1 Corinthians 15:56). The worst part about death, the stinger that makes us throb with pain, is that it's our fault. It really is "on us and on our children."

> If the cross is necessary to save us, then *what did we do?*

We bear a boatload of guilt, and we must own it. It won't do to conceal our guilt with euphemisms that let us off the hook. Some Christians take the edge off sin by describing it as "brokenness" or the "junk in our lives." Others define sin as "mistakes" that set us up to "find failure and disappointment in our relationships." Brokenness and junk may be symptoms of our sin, but such cheap substitutes don't begin to assess the underlying rebellion that causes our mistakes, failure, and disappointment.

Our sin goes all the way down, and unless we admit that we cannot be saved. The angel told Joseph to name his Son "Jesus," not because He will deliver His people from sadness or low self-esteem but "because he will save his people from their sins" (Matthew 1:21). Jesus accepted this mission and announced, "I have not come to call the righteous, but sinners to repentance" (Luke 5:32). Jesus died for sinners who desperately need His help, and unless we concede we are those sinners, His sacrifice will not heal us.

Here are the facts. Adam and Eve disobeyed God when they ate from the one tree he told them not to. They immediately felt guilty and ashamed, so they covered themselves with fig leaves and hid among the trees of the garden. Since resisting God—who is life—is the shortest path to death, God told them they would die, "for dust you are and to dust you will return" (Genesis 3:19).

We join their rebellion when we thumb our nose at God, doing what we want when we want and not allowing anyone, especially God, to cramp our style. We also join their penalty, "for the wages of sin is death" (Romans 6:23). Martin Luther observed that "death is a penalty; therefore it is something sad." He added, "I don't like to see examples of joyful death. On the other hand, I like to see those who tremble and shake and grow pale when they face death and yet get through. It was so with the great saints; they were not glad to die."

Perhaps you wonder whether death remains a punishment for the follower of Jesus Christ. Didn't Jesus pay the penalty on our behalf when he "redeemed us from the curse of the law by becoming a curse for us"? (Galatians 3:13). As one theologian concludes, death for Christians is no longer "a consequence of sin."

This doesn't seem to fit our experience. Jesus has forgiven our sin, but He hasn't yet removed all of its consequences. As a repentant chain smoker may still die of lung cancer and a reformed philanderer may still die from an HIV infection, so a forgiven sinner must still suffer the consequences of his or her sin. And if one of the consequences is a dreadful thing like death, it's hard to take this as anything other than a penalty.

The bad news is we die and it's our fault. We can't shake it off and keep going, for our sin is real and a very big deal. The good news is that while we were running away from our guilt, Jesus was running toward it. He "was pierced for our transgressions, he was crushed for our iniquities; the punishment that brought us peace was upon him, and by his wounds we are healed" (Isaiah 53:5). Jesus joined us in the punishment we deserved, for if we were going to be delivered from the guilt and penalty of death, it would have to be an inside job. "The wages of sin is death," Paul says, "but the gift of God is eternal life in Christ Jesus our Lord" (Romans 6:23).

> While we were running away from our guilt, Jesus was running toward it.

Questions for Reflection

1. Do you think you deserve to die?

2. If Jesus paid the penalty for our sin, then why do we still die?

3. Is "brokenness" a suitable synonym for sin?

4. Why is it essential that we admit the extent of our rebellion? What problems arise when we fail to acknowledge the depth of our sin?

TEN

ENEMY

The last enemy to be destroyed is death.

1 Corinthians 15:26

IN THE SPRING OF 1910, King Edward VII of England caught a cold over a chilly and rainy weekend. Ignoring his doctors by refusing to rest, the popular king developed bronchitis, then pneumonia, and was dead by Friday. His funeral was preached by Henry Scott-Holland, the canon of St. Paul's Cathedral, who uttered these venerable lines, which were largely forgotten until they were discovered decades later by Ann Landers.

The canon spoke on behalf of the king:

> Death is nothing at all. I have only slipped away into the next room. . . . Life means all that it ever meant. It is the same as it ever was. There is absolute unbroken continuity. What is death but a negligible accident? Why should I be out of mind because I am out of sight? I am waiting for you for an interval. Somewhere very near. Just around the corner. All is well. Nothing is past; nothing is

lost. One brief moment and all will be as it was before. How we shall laugh at the trouble of parting when we meet again!

These sentimental words, so frequently shared at funerals, are over their head in denial. Does anyone really believe that "death is nothing at all," nothing "but a negligible accident"? If it were, would so many strain so hard to prove it's nothing? We saw our culture's feeble attempts to neutralize death: It's really not so bad because we'll meld into some divine force or energy, linger in someone's memory, or at least we won't be any worse off than before we were born. These platitudes leave us grasping for more, and so we frequently hear two other reasons why death is better than we think.

Some say death is necessary for life to have meaning. If our lives never ended, we couldn't wrap them up and say whether they were good or bad. Athletic contests must end to have winners and losers, performances must conclude before we can applaud, sentences must finish to understand what was said, and we must die to put a period on our lives.

I agree that closure is necessary to evaluate a body of work. A book or song that never ends would be difficult to review. "I like it so far," is all we could offer. "I'll say more when this incessant thing is over!" Likewise, this life must end so we can stand before the judgment seat of Christ. But why must it end in death? We know that those who are alive when Jesus returns will achieve closure without dying, so death is not the only way this life could end. Closure, not death, is necessary to find meaning.

And not always even that. Someday we will live forever with Jesus on the New Earth. We will enjoy discrete moments of closure, finishing this meal and that conversation, but we will never die. Will our immortality create an existential crisis? Will we pull our hair in despair and cry, "Why Lord?

What does my unending life even mean?" If not, why should we think death is necessary to find meaning?

Some quit these half-hearted rationalizations and go for broke. Elisabeth Kübler-Ross was a pioneer in the study of death and famously gave us the five stages of grief: denial, anger, bargaining, depression, and acceptance. She herself seemed stuck on the first stage, for she claimed that death is actually a step up for the soul: "When people die, they very simply shed their body, much as a butterfly comes out of its cocoon." For Kübler-Ross, death is merely a door into a higher state of consciousness where we continue to play, laugh, and grow.

This romanticized notion of death is the dominant view in our culture. Most people think that everyone who dies continues to do the things they love, only better and in heaven. Weekend golfers are suddenly hitting all the celestial fairways, middling musicians are jamming in heaven's band, and people who were pains in the neck here are *really* annoying up there. The problem with such amusingly comforting thoughts is they have no basis in reality. The only reason to believe them is that we want them to be true. But wanting something to be true does not make it true. This popular view of heaven is about as likely as Santa Claus.

But isn't Kübler-Ross right to think death is an improvement? Don't Christians believe that death is a graduation into our glorious existence in heaven? A friend was sharing the counsel he gave teenagers whose Christian friend had died in a car accident. "Don't forget," he said, "Melissa's death is a tragedy for you and her family, but for her it's a good thing."

I stopped my friend. "I understand what you are trying to say," I told him, "but it's not quite right. Praise God that He brings good things out of death, but death itself is not a good thing. Paul said that death is our last enemy, the very thing that Jesus came to destroy."

I don't think my friend completely agreed with me, and perhaps you are wondering too. Didn't Paul say that "to die is gain," for then he would "depart and be with Christ"? (Philippians 1:21–23). Paul desperately wanted to see Jesus, and if it was the best deal he could get, he was willing to die to make it happen. But his first choice was to be with Jesus without enduring the ordeal of death. Paul signed his letters with the prayer "Maranatha," which means "Come, O Lord!" (1 Corinthians 16:22). Paul believed that it's worth dying to be with Jesus, but he preferred to skip death and simply welcome Jesus back to our planet.

> Praise God that He brings good things out of death, but death itself is not a good thing.

But isn't death a good thing in Psalm 116:15, which says, "Precious in the sight of the Lord is the death of his saints"? This verse does not mean death itself is precious to God, but that our death is important to Him because we are. Like a mother who mourns the death of her son or a colonel who honors the casualties from his regiment, God takes our death personally. Psalm 116 is a song of praise to God who "delivered my soul from death" (v. 8). The psalmist rests in the comfort that the gracious God who rescued him once will rock him to sleep when he eventually dies.

We must not confuse the good that God brings out of death with death itself. Often people who are facing death say their cancer was the best thing that ever happened to them. They mean that the cancer stopped them in their tracks and shocked them into reevaluating their priorities, and now they are spending more time with their kids and focusing on things that matter. But note that it's their right response to the cancer, not the cancer itself, that is the good thing. Their impending death is unmistakably evil. How else could it shake them awake?

I once attended the funeral of an infant who had died in a tragic accident. The pastor offered the usual words of comfort: "We can rejoice, for this child is better off than we are. He isn't really dead. He is more alive than he's ever been, safe in the arms of Jesus." There is precious truth in these words, though they seemed to skate past the grief of the numb parents. Couldn't we acknowledge that something horrible had happened?

> Sin is the enemy that will one day steal from us everything and everyone we have ever loved.

I appreciated more the words of the grieving father, who with quivering voice declared that no parent should ever have to bury their child. He pointed out that every death is ultimately the result of sin, and that when he held his dead son in the hospital, he thought he saw the face of sin. The mask of sin had been ripped away and he saw sin for what it is, the enemy that will one day steal from us everything and everyone we have ever loved.

The father didn't try to make us believe that all was well, but from the depths of despair he raised a fist of defiance. "People tell me that someday I will make peace with Jack's death," he said. "I will *never* be at peace with death. Scripture tells me that one day I will be at peace, but only when death is no more. I will not be at peace until I see my son again."

That is the Christian view of death.

Questions for Reflection

1. If a friend quoted to you Henry Scott-Holland's words, "Death is nothing at all. . . . All is well," how would you respond?

2. Is death a good thing for the Christian?

3. Why do most people say that their loved ones are now in heaven, doing perfectly whatever they enjoyed doing on earth? What reason do they have for thinking this is true?

4. If our loved ones are right now golfing and riding horses in heaven, then is a future resurrection even needed?

5. When is death defeated: when we die and go to heaven or when Jesus returns and raises us from the dead?

PART TWO

TRUST CHRIST'S VICTORY

ELEVEN

CRUCIFIXION

Christ redeemed us from the curse of the law by
becoming a curse for us.

Galatians 3:13

IMMACULÉE ILIBAGIZA ESCAPED the genocide in Rwanda by
crouching with six women in a three foot by four foot bathroom for three months. Outside the walls of their safe house,
one million of their Tutsi tribe were being slaughtered by
their Hutu neighbors. Immaculée expected to die—eventually one of the machete-wielding thugs scouring their house
would look in the bathroom—and she begged God for courage to face her brutal end.

Immaculée experienced in a horribly heightened way
what we all should feel when we consider our predicament.
She trembled with terror when Hutus entered her house,
when one put his hand on the bathroom door and another
shouted her name. She was waiting for a literal grim reaper, a
man with a machete who might come at any moment to end
her life.

We may not be cramped and hiding, but we live under a
similar sentence of death. As poet W. S. Merwin observed,

every year we pass unaware the anniversary of our death. That fact would grip us with fear if we stopped to think about it. Death is the big zero that negates everything. Did the man of your dreams just ask you to marry him? Did your beloved Cubs finally win the World Series? Were you honored as executive of the year for the Association of Middle Managers for Midwestern Mutual Insurance Companies, Northwest Ohio District? None of this will matter when you're dead (some of it may not matter even now!). Regardless of how high you fly, you will always come down, for one day you will lie flat on your back, stone-cold dead. And then you will disappear entirely from this life, soon to be forgotten.

Death makes life absurd. We are foolish to get excited over blue skies, homemade bread, making the honor roll, the birth of a child, a touchdown pass, or a swelling portfolio. We are foolish to care at all—unless something even more foolish has broken into our absurd world. What if something happened in our hopeless world that, because it was even more hopeless, bottomed out our despair and pulled us back toward hope? What if there is something even more foolish than death?

This is what Christians have always believed about God. Our almighty Creator loved us so much that He crossed an infinite chasm to become one of us, and when He arrived He disappointed nearly everyone. Jesus' own family thought He was crazy and did not believe in Him (Mark 3:21; John 7:5). The crowds hung around Jesus for the free food and magic show, but they dispersed with groans when Jesus explained that He had come from heaven to save the world. Even His disciples shook their heads in disbelief, saying, "This is a hard teaching. Who can accept it?" (John 6:60).

Jesus looked at the Twelve who were left and asked, "You do not want to leave too, do you?" Peter reassured his Lord,

"We believe and know that you are the Holy One of God" (John 6:67–69), though it wouldn't be long until he and his companions also became disillusioned.

The disciples expected Jesus to lead the armies of heaven against Caesar, freeing the Jews from their Roman overlord. Their revolutionary dreams seemed to be coming true when Jesus triumphantly entered Jerusalem, though even that was a bit ridiculous. Who rides a donkey into the capital to claim His throne? Perhaps to force a showdown with the authorities and to replenish the money he had stolen, Judas betrayed his Lord for thirty pieces of silver.

There were darker forces at work, as Satan entered Judas for this climactic battle with the King (John 13:27). Satan had gained authority over the world and its human caretakers when he tempted Adam and Eve to rebel against God. He presided over a foolish and decaying kingdom of sin and death, but at least he was in charge. He knew that Jesus had come to end his reign as "the prince of this world" (John 12:31), and he was willing to deal. Satan offered to give Jesus the world if only He would do the rational thing—tip His hat in gratitude for this special offer. But Jesus would not bow to anyone except His heavenly Father (Matthew 4:10). Realizing that Jesus refused to be reasonable, Satan decided Jesus would have to die.

Here the story becomes powerfully absurd, and absurdly powerful. Paul explained that "the message of the cross is foolishness to those who are perishing, but to us who are being saved it is the power of God" (1 Corinthians 1:18). Nothing is more preposterous than the Son of God dying on a cross, falsely accused, stripped, whipped, and then strung up to suffer excruciating pain, the jeers from His executioners, and the betrayal of the One who had sent Him on this mission. Yet nothing else can undercut the absurdity of death.

God was never weaker than in that painful, pivotal afternoon. Jesus didn't even bring a knife to this gunfight, for when Peter drew his sword to defend his Lord, Jesus told him, "Put your sword away! Shall I not drink the cup the Father has given me?" (John 18:11). The earth shuddered as demons danced around the cross, shrieking in glee as the Son of God screamed, "My God, my God, why have you forsaken me?" (Matthew 27:46).

But God's weakest point was also His greatest show of force, for His suffering was powerfully bearing our sin away, "nailing it to the cross. And having disarmed the powers and authorities, he made a public spectacle of them, triumphing over them by the cross" (Colossians 2:14–15). God was never stronger than when He hung on the cross, for His foolish death absorbed the absurdity of sin and brought "life for all men" (Romans 5:18).

> God was never stronger than when He hung on the cross, for His death brought "life for all men."

C. S. Lewis described how the foolishness of the cross deceived the devil and broke the power of sin and death. In *The Lion, the Witch, and the Wardrobe*, Aslan, who signifies the Lion of Judah, had come back to life after offering his life to the White Witch so that Edmund could go free.

"But what does it all mean?" asked Susan.

Aslan replied,

> It means that though the Witch knew the Deep Magic [that everyone must die for their sins], there is a magic deeper still which she did not know. Her knowledge goes back only to the dawn of Time. But if she could have looked a little further back, into the stillness and the darkness before Time dawned, she

would have read there a different incantation. She would have known that when a willing victim who had committed no treachery was killed in a traitor's stead, the Table would crack and Death itself would start working backward.

This marvelously strange truth of the cross inspired Immaculée as she endured her own bizarre predicament. Locked for months in her stifling cell, eating bug-infested beans and waiting for death, Immaculée read how Peter learned to put down his sword and "follow in [the] steps" of the One who "bore our sins in his body on the tree" (1 Peter 2:21, 24). She felt the Lord say, "I am your example. I have gone before you, and I have shown you how to face death and handle anything that happens to you." She embraced the reckless grace of the cross, and when later she met the killer of her mother and brother, she offered the unimaginable words of life, "I forgive you."

Ninety-one days after her ordeal began, a gaunt but grateful Immaculée found shelter in a refugee camp. Her life was spared, at least for now. Unless Jesus returns, Immaculée will eventually die like everyone else, but her death will be different because of the cross. Death itself is in retreat, for death has died in the death of Jesus Christ. The specter of death may continue to haunt, but the permanent fix is underway. Death is already working backward.

> Death itself is in retreat, for death has died in the death of Jesus Christ.

Questions for Reflection

1. Would you like to know the day and time when you are going to die?

2. Why is death absurd? How does death make life absurd?

3. How is the cross both God's weakest and strongest point?

4. Are you disappointed with God? How might that be a reflection on you rather than God?

TWELVE

RESURRECTION

He was delivered over to death for our sins and
was raised to life for our justification.

Romans 4:25

MARCUS BORG AND N. T. (TOM) WRIGHT are leading theologians for their respective liberal and conservative sides. They
aired their differences in the book *The Meaning of Jesus*, which
they promoted with friendly debates about who Jesus is and
whether He had risen from the dead. In one of those debates,
Borg said it was hard to believe that Jesus' dead body came to
life and walked away. "I just can't imagine how such a thing
could happen," he confessed. Wright turned to his friend
and said, "I think you need to enlarge your imagination!" We
shouldn't be surprised that history's most important event is
also its most spectacular.

Borg needlessly closes his mind to the resurrection. He
starts from the secular premise that science explains all, and
since scientists have never seen God or a resurrection, he
concludes that Jesus is not God and did not rise from the
dead. Instead, Borg argues that the resurrection is merely a
"powerfully true metaphor" for the experience of the early
Christians. Their memory of Jesus was so strong that they

often sensed He was still with them—a feeling they expressed by saying the spirit of Jesus had risen from the tomb.

Borg's take on the resurrection would have infuriated the early church. They weren't claiming that the spirit of their departed leader lived on, as other religions claim of their leaders, but that their dead Savior had physically come to life and left His empty tomb. He had not merely gone on, He had come back. He had kicked down the door of death and come out the other side. The early Christians saw and touched Jesus' breathing, resurrection body, and they believed he was alive, like you and me, only more so.

Liberal Christians such as Borg mistakenly think they can keep the *meaning* of the resurrection without believing in the *fact* of the resurrection. They don't believe Jesus bodily rose from the dead, yet they insist that the resurrection that did not happen can still inspire us today. Liberal pastors babble on in their Easter sermons about the promise of spring, the love that conquers all, and the hope that tomorrow will be better than today. They encourage us to keep the spirit of Jesus alive by following His example: feeding the poor, comforting the sick, and keeping the faith during our darkest hours.

But if Jesus is dead, what's the point? Paul explains, "If Christ has not been raised, our preaching is useless and so is your faith." Take away the resurrection of Jesus and you take away all hope. Take away the resurrection and "we are to be pitied more than all men" (1 Corinthians 15:14–19).

Conservative Christians may also stop short on the resurrection. Our mistake is less than the liberals, but what happened Easter morning is also larger than we think. We often regard the resurrection of Jesus as nothing more than evidence that the cross took. We are saved from sin by the cross, and we know that for sure because Jesus rose from the dead. We assume a simple, one-on-one matchup: the cross defeats sin and the resurrection overcomes death, guaranteeing that we will live forever with God. We read the resurrection like the last line of a children's story, where everyone "lived happily ever after." Jesus' resurrection adds nothing essential to our salvation; it merely assures us that everything turned out in the end.

And the end is usually understood to be heaven, where our weary souls go after they have shed the burden of their bodies. A recent Scripps Howard poll found that barely half of "born again" Christians believe their physical bodies will live again. The rest believe their souls will live forever, but this is much less than the biblical hope for the resurrection of the body. Have we really conquered death if our souls must live forever without our bodies? It seems that death has won something important, for without a resurrection we won't be the whole persons we were before we died.

We can't appreciate how Jesus' resurrection defeats death unless we understand how it conquers sin. The resurrection is more than the defining miracle that proves Jesus is God and the gospel is true. Paul declares that the resurrection is a vital piece of the gospel, for Jesus "was raised to life for our justification" (Romans 4:25), and "if Christ has not been raised, your faith is futile; you are still in your sins" (1 Corinthians 15:17). Here's why.

Incomplete View		How Jesus' Resurrection Saves Us from Sin and Death	
Cross	Resurrection	Creation	Resurrection: Father releases Jesus (and us) from our penalty
↓	↓	↓	↑
Sin	Death	Fall: sin and death ⟶	Cross: Jesus bore our penalty of sin and death

Adam and Eve plunged us all into sin and death when they overstepped their boundary and tried to become like God. A wise parent establishes new limits when boundaries are crossed—putting their unruly toddler in a corner or grounding their disobedient teenager—so God punished our transgression with the new limit of death. We may kick and scream as God carries us from the room, but we cannot pretend we are in charge. The sweeper arm of death flattens high and low alike and reminds us of the infinite boundary between us and God.

We cannot cross this boundary and we shouldn't even try—that's how we got into this mess. But the boundary was crossed from the other direction. God was big enough to stoop low and squeeze into our world. The Son of God "did not consider equality with God something to be grasped," so He "made himself nothing, taking the very nature of a servant, being made in human likeness. And being found in appearance as a man, he humbled himself and became obedient to death—even death on a cross!" (Philippians 2:6–8).

On the cross Jesus bore the penalty of our sin and death. Paul explains that "God made him who had no sin to be sin for us, so that in him we might become the righteousness of God" (2 Corinthians 5:21). God punished Jesus on the cross, and if the story ends there, Jesus remains punished with us. He continues to bear the penalty of our sin. He remains guilty, and so are we. And if we remain in our sin, we will remain in our graves.

The resurrection is the Father's glorious vindication of His beloved Son. On Easter morning, the Father reversed His verdict, announcing to the world that He accepted Jesus' sacrifice and released Him from the guilt and punishment of our sin. Since the punishment of sin is death, God raised His exonerated Son "from the dead, freeing him from the agony of death, because it was impossible for death to keep its hold on him" (Acts 2:24).

What is true about Jesus is also true about all who identify with Him. Jesus died as our substitute—*instead* of us; but He rose as our representative—*with* us. Jesus died in our place, so we won't pay for sin. He rose to establish our place, so we will live again. Our sin was buried with Jesus and left behind when the Father raised Him from the grave. Now we who put our faith in Jesus are counted righteous with Him, so that "just as Christ was raised from the dead through the glory of the Father, we too may live a new life" (Romans 6:4).

> The resurrection is the recovery of the life we enjoyed before our death.

This new life is so much more than an ethereal, partial existence where we learn to make do without our bodies, for it is nothing less than the restoration of God's originally good creation. The resurrection is more than a guarantee of life after death; it is the recovery of the life we enjoyed before our death, with all of its evil removed. We may still die, but Jesus' resurrection means death is no longer a dead end. There is life after death, and it's here, where we will live forever with Jesus as whole people on God's New Earth.

Easter morning is the sunrise on a whole new world. Jesus came back from the dead, and if you repent of your sin and believe in Him, so will you.

Questions for Reflection

1. Can you think of anything more incredible than a dead person coming back to life? How do you know that the resurrection of Jesus actually happened?

2. Why is the *fact* of Jesus' resurrection necessary for its *meaning* to be true?

3. Why is Jesus' resurrection necessary for our sins to be forgiven?

4. Why must Christians believe that their bodies will rise from the dead? Why isn't it enough to say that our spirits will live forever in heaven?

THIRTEEN

TRIUMPH

But thanks be to God! He gives us the victory
through our Lord Jesus Christ.

1 Corinthians 15:57

THE STADIUM SHOOK WITH cheers as the elderly Polycarp
appeared before the Roman governor. "Have respect to your
old age," the governor begged the bishop of Smyrna. "Swear
by the genius of Caesar and say, 'Away with the atheists!'"
(The Romans believed the Christians were atheists because
their God was invisible.)

Polycarp waved his hand toward the clamoring pagans
and joked, "Away with the atheists!"

The governor ignored the insult and tried again: "Swear,
and I release you. Curse Christ."

Polycarp replied, "Eighty-six years have I served him, and
he has done me no wrong: how then can I blaspheme my
King who saved me?"

The governor threatened to feed Polycarp to the lions.
Polycarp said bring them on. The governor said he would have
him burned. Polycarp told him to hurry. As they bound his
arms behind his back, just before they lit the match, Polycarp

shouted thanks to God for considering him "worthy of this day and hour; that I might take a portion among the martyrs in the cup of Christ, to the resurrection of eternal life."

Such courage in the face of death could only arise from Polycarp's confidence in the resurrected Christ. Jesus emboldened the first Christians by dying the worst possible death and living to tell about it. He took death's best shot, got up off the mat, and floored death with a straight cross. He drug death down with Him into the depths, and when He arose He left death in the dust. Jesus now stands over death and glowers, "Is that all you got?"

> Jesus took death's best shot, got up off the mat, and floored death with a straight cross.

This disdain for death empowered the persecuted apostles to rejoice that "they had been counted worthy of suffering disgrace for the Name" of Christ (Acts 5:41). Paul declared, "I consider my life worth nothing to me, if only I may finish the race and complete the task the Lord Jesus has given me—the task of testifying to the gospel of God's grace" (Acts 20:24).

Paul's view inspired Ignatius, the bishop of Antioch, to eagerly anticipate his martyrdom. He wrote, "I am God's wheat, and I am being ground by the teeth of the beasts so that I may appear as pure bread." He explained that he was "longing for death," for to remain alive was actually a form of death and to die was really to be born into life. He said, "It is glorious to have my sunset from the world but towards God, that I may have my sunrise to him."

I appreciate Ignatius's desire to depart and be with Jesus, but he seems to overlook that our triumph over death, like redemption itself, is not complete when we die but occurs in two stages. God created us with both *physical* and *spiritual* life. Our fall destroyed both forms of life, for our sin brings physical death and also severs our relationship with God. A holy God cannot commune with sinners; He stopped walking with Adam and Eve in the garden of Eden after their rebellion. Redemption restores both our spiritual and physical life, though not equally or at the same time.

First, redemption restores our spiritual life. We become spiritually alive when we commit our lives to Christ, for we are "born again, not of perishable seed, but of imperishable, through the living and enduring word of God" (1 Peter 1:23). Our spiritual seed bursts into full bloom the moment we die because our souls immediately enter the glorious presence of God. This led the early Christians to call the day of their death their *dies natalis,* or day of their birth, and it explains Jesus' paradox that "he who believes in me will live, even though he dies; and whoever lives and believes in me will never die" (John 11:25).

What precious comfort to know that we will never fully die! Jesus has so thoroughly defeated death that death now works for Him. Our punishment for sin has become a door to life, for when we fall asleep here we awake in glory over there. Death may not be good, but it is gain, for it brings us to God. This is part of what Paul meant when he exclaimed that Jesus "has destroyed death and has brought life and immortality to light through the gospel" (2 Timothy 1:10).

> Death may not be good, but it is gain, for it brings us to God.

Next, redemption restores our physical bodies. Our resurrection is an earthy, material promise. The same power that restores our spiritual life will also restore our physical life, for the God "who raised Christ from the dead will also give life to your mortal bodies through his Spirit, who lives in you" (Romans 8:11). Redemption doesn't partially restore creation, renewing our spiritual life at the expense of our physical existence. The resurrection targets our bodies, which is God's way of letting us know that all of life—in its spiritual and physical fullness—will be restored.

With this in mind, a Christian funeral does at least two things. First, we mourn the loss of our loved one. There is an empty spot at our table, in our church, and in our home. We also mourn for ourselves, for we miss our loved one terribly and we realize that someday we will be the person in the casket. Death is a patient, stubborn enemy. It survives longer than Satan and is the last thing thrown into the lake of fire (Revelation 20:10, 14). We know that someday it will come for us.

Second, and this is crucial, we raise a fist of defiance. It appears that death has won. Death has snatched our loved one and she is never coming back. But we know better than to trust our eyes, and we choose to allow the Word of God to interpret what we see. God's Word assures us that death does not have the last word, for our loved one who has died in Christ is alive and with the Lord. What is more, any day now Jesus will return with our loved one, raise her body, and restore her to the full vitality of her spiritual and physical life. He may do it before we leave the cemetery.

So we refuse to live in fear. Like a clever horror movie, death frightens with suspense, shadows, and slamming doors. We shake and shudder as we imagine what monster lurks around the corner. As Luther said, the "fear of death, despair, terror is death itself." Jesus' resurrection flipped on the lights, stopped the chilly soundtrack, and ripped the mask off death. We realize that death means us harm, but even its worst turns out for our best, for when it kills it brings us to life. Death may be evil, but it's serving God now.

So raise your voice and join Paul's triumphant taunt, "Where, O death, is your victory? Where, O death, is your sting?" (1 Corinthians 15:55). Don't believe what you see, but trust only what you hear from God's Word. The grave where you say goodbye is resurrection ground.

Questions for Reflection

1. How does the fact that Jesus triumphed over death encourage you as you prepare to die?

2. What does the resurrection imply about the importance of your body and your earthly, physical life?

3. Which is more frightening to you, the act of dying or the idea of dying?

4. Besides celebrating the life of the deceased, what else must a Christian funeral do?

FOURTEEN

REST

I am the resurrection and the life. . . . Do you
believe this?

John 11:25–26

ED DOBSON HAD BEEN diagnosed with ALS, and he was wrestling with the fears that come from such news as he preached
a sermon series on stewardship. One Sunday he spoke about
how the Christians in Corinth first gave themselves to the
Lord, and he asked an usher to bring him an offering plate.
He told the congregation that when the ushers passed the
plates that morning, everyone should have put the plate on
the floor and stood in it. Then he placed his plate on the
floor, stepped inside, and preached the rest of the sermon
from there.

After the service Ed pondered the question he had asked
his people, "What part of your life is not in the plate?" He
realized he had been holding out on God. He had committed his waning arms and legs, but he had not yet relinquished
control over his tongue. So he told God, "I give you my speak-
ing. If this is the last sermon I ever preach, it's okay with me."
The peace of surrender swept over Ed, and for the first time

since his diagnosis he felt he had given every part of his life to God. Surrender is not a one-off event, and Ed candidly confesses that he often wants to climb back out of the plate. He must continually pray, "God, I surrender myself and my future completely to you."

Surrender—giving ourselves entirely to Christ—is the only way to live, so it's not surprising that surrender is also the best way to die. Resting in Jesus alone is precisely how we join His victory over sin and death.

Scripture symbolizes sin and death as a deep, dark sea. The ocean is a dangerous place; its stormy swells swallow ships and drag their crews down into the abyss, where they are never seen or heard again. God connected death to the sea in his questions to Job: "Have you journeyed to the springs of the sea or walked in the recesses of the deep? Have the gates of death been shown to you? Have you seen the gates of the shadow of death?" (Job 38:16–17). David compared death to a tempestuous sea: "The waves of death swirled about me; the torrents of destruction overwhelmed me" (2 Samuel 22:5). When Jesus wanted to frighten His audience, He told them they would be worse off than a man who had "a large mill-stone hung around his neck" and was "drowned in the depths of the sea" (Matthew 18:6). John's Revelation explains that the Beast is evil by saying he came out of the sea, and it depicts the absence of evil and death on the New Earth by declaring "there was no longer any sea" (Revelation 13:1; 21:1).

To continue the metaphor of the sea as death, our sin has shipwrecked our lives and cast us into an ocean of despair. We instinctively splash and kick as we struggle to stay afloat, but the harder we swim the sooner we tire and drown. The only way to survive in open water is to relax, use your natural buoyancy to stay afloat, and wait for help to arrive. That's easier said than done, especially when you have no idea if anyone knows you're drowning. It's hard to stay calm when all you see is dark, briny sea.

The normal, frenetic arc of life goes something like this. Young people don't tend to think much about death, so they spend their early years chasing fun and yearning for a calling that will help others and possibly change the world. Their idealism is doused by the cold reality of competition and the need to be responsible, and soon enough they begin to seek their significance in the smaller worlds of family, work, and wealth.

By mid-career they realize that riches and respect won't matter when they're dead, and they turn their attention to prolonging their lives. The aging take drugs and get injections, rub on creams and use dyes, and try diets and surgeries to appear younger and more fit. The highest compliment they can be paid is "You don't look your age." But they *are* their age, and eventually they die of some complication or other, leaving whatever prestige and possessions they have accumulated to the next generation. As they depart, they sigh with Solomon, "And who knows whether [my heir] will be a wise man or a fool? Yet he will have control over all the work into which I have poured my effort and skill under the sun" (Ecclesiastes 2:19).

Such ends the doomed life of everyone who does not know God. The great news of the gospel is that we don't have to do the impossible and spin something out of the unraveling yarn of life, for Jesus has rescued us with the jujutsu of the cross. Jujutsu teaches that it is unwise to trade blows with a bully who is larger than you, but by yielding and pivoting you can use your attacker's weight and energy against him. The Son of God used this technique when He became a vulnerable human, susceptible to death, "so that by his death he might destroy him who holds the power of death—that is, the devil"

(Hebrews 2:14). Jesus allowed death to take Him down so he could take death out. He turned death's sword back on itself; death died in the death of Christ.

Christ's victory through defeat became the rallying cry of the Christian martyrs. As Polycarp entered the raucous stadium, "there came a voice to him from heaven, 'Be strong, Polycarp, and play the man.'" Polycarp bravely battled the forces of evil, which he conquered by allowing them to do as they wished. His jujutsu unmasked the authorities, for by submitting to them he signaled that their power was too weak to bother resisting. He couldn't muster the interest to fight back; they just weren't worth the effort.

> Jesus allowed death to take Him down so he could take death out.

Polycarp's followers made the same point when they announced that he had been "arrested by Herod" but died "in the everlasting reign of Jesus Christ; to whom be honor, glory, dominion, and an everlasting throne from generation to generation." They collected Polycarp's bones and vowed to "celebrate the birthday of his martyrdom, alike in memory of them that have fought before, and for the training and preparation of them that are to fight hereafter."

> We rest when it's our time to go because we are already resting on the promises of God.

We fight alongside Polycarp and in Christ when we imitate his cruciform jujutsu. Rather than beg and bargain before the onslaught of death, we rest when it's our time to go because we are already resting on the promises of God. We have surrendered our entire selves to Christ, and so we are free to surrender to death, which no longer has any power over us. Paul explains that "since Christ was raised from the dead, he cannot die again; death no longer has mastery over him" (Romans 6:9). If by faith we are in Christ, the same is true of us.

We practice our jujutsu move on death every night when we go to bed. There is a reason centuries of children offered this bedtime prayer: "Now I lay me down to sleep, I pray the Lord my soul to keep. And if I die before I wake, I pray the Lord my soul to take." Sleep is great preparation for death, which it closely resembles. Every night we must choose to trust God with the demands of the next day. We clear our minds and cleanse our hearts by casting all our cares upon Him, which frees us to drift into deep and dreamy slumber. If we have trained ourselves to fall asleep at bedtime, we will be more than ready to fall victoriously into the sleep of death.

Do you believe the promise of God? Then go to bed, and sleep on it.

Questions for Reflection

1. Why is the sea a fitting metaphor for death?

2. What bothers you the most about aging?

3. How is surrendering to death the only way to defeat death?

4. Why is bedtime an opportunity to prepare for your moment of death? Write a bedtime prayer that you can recite as you prepare for your final breath.

FIFTEEN

REPENT

I have been crucified with Christ and I no longer
live, but Christ lives in me.

Galatians 2:20

I WAS FLIPPING CHANNELS during my workout when I caught
this snippet on an afternoon talk show. The host noticed that
television star Ray Romano had mentioned he was fifty-three
years old, and she asked whether he was worried about growing older.

"Of course," he responded. "I'm a comedian, so I'm neu-
rotic about everything. But I've decided to tell myself I'm
going to live forever. I try not to think about death; it's easier
that way."

In a moment of comedic honesty, Romano added, "I would
like death to sneak up on me. I want to be shot by a sniper, so
I don't even see it coming. I want it to be a good sniper, not a
weekend sniper who is slightly off target, because that would
raise a whole new set of problems. But death by sniper would
be the way to go."

Romano jokingly expressed what many people secretly
wish. The best they can hope for is to become rich and famous,

travel to exotic beaches, feast on foreign foods with unpronounceable names, get box seats, enjoy amazing sex, and—just as they are sucking the last bit of marrow out of life—depart this world in a sudden, unforeseen instant.

This wish makes sense, but it seems selfish. The deceased may perish too quickly to feel fear or pain, but what about the loved ones they leave behind? Who would want to burden friends and family with the trauma of their sudden exit? This wish is also lethal, for Jesus said, "Whoever wants to save his life will lose it" (Matthew 16:25). Romano concedes his endgame is a total loss—that's why he wants it to come quickly and without warning. But his loss is even larger than he knows, for the person who lives for himself forfeits his own soul.

Rather than live now only to die later, Jesus invites us to die so we can live both now and forever. He urges us to take up our cross and follow Him. He promises, "whoever loses his life for me will find it" (Matthew 16:24–25).

> Rather than live now only to die later, Jesus invites us to die so we can live both now and forever.

Death means the end of self. We all have dreams and desires, goals that promise to satisfy our deepest longings. Complete this sentence: *I will be perfectly happy and content when* _____. When we're young, we think the free time of summer is just what we need, but by August we're bored and missing our friends and the structure of school. As we mature, we imagine our life will come together when we marry, then have children (what were we thinking?), then grandchildren (that's better). We believe we'll be fulfilled when we land our dream job, then earn a promotion, then make six figures, then pay off the mortgage, then save enough to retire early. When we finally retire, we think we'll be satisfied if we travel and hang out with friends, then if we travel to better places with better friends, and then we realize we're going to die soon anyway so what does it really matter?

These goals are more or less good, but if they become our ultimate aims, the saviors that will make our lives worth living, then we are asking more from them than they can deliver. We inevitably turn them into little gods that can't bear our weight. If we lean on them, they will collapse, destroying both us and them.

Two facts are always true about idols. First, idols serve their makers, so it is we who pray and put our hope in them who actually play the role of god. We are in charge, and they exist to meet our needs. Second, idols wear us out. As the Philistines rose each morning to dust off and prop up their fallen god Dagon (1 Samuel 5:1–5), so we discover that idols demand our constant care and protection.

Here's a question to determine whether your God is true: *Who is carrying whom?* If you are continually fretting over your god and must load him on your shoulders and carry him out of harm's way, then you have an idol. You are playing the exhausting role of God. But if you find you can put all your weight on the object of your worship and can curl up and fall asleep in the middle of any storm, then congratulations, you have come to the end of yourself and are serving the one, true God.

The liberating news of the gospel is that everyone who believes in Jesus has died with Him from the need to play God. Paul explains, "I have been crucified with Christ and I no longer live, but Christ lives in me" (Galatians 2:20), and he informs his fellow Christians that "you died, and your life is now hidden with Christ in God" (Colossians 3:3). Jesus died *instead* of us but *not without* us. Karl Barth elaborates, "That Jesus Christ died for us does not mean, therefore, that we do not have to die, but that we have died in and with him, that as the people we were we have been done away and destroyed, that we are no longer there and have no more future."

It's a relief to learn we have died with Christ, for dead people don't have to pretend they are God. They are relieved of the responsibility to create and sustain their lives. They feel no pressure to keep things going, for their life is already over. An ordinary person who is blessed with success just might wish for a sniper to ease his burden by suddenly snatching it all away. But those who have died with Christ have nothing more to lose. Death has no leverage over people who are already dead.

> Death has no leverage over people who are already dead.

In this way, spiritual death is excellent preparation for physical death. If we have come to the end of ourselves spiritually and are no longer focused on our personal fulfillment, then it won't be the end of the world when we die physically, for we weren't living for ourselves anyway. When we begin each day with the confession that we aren't God, we build stamina for the day we go to be with God.

What is more, the surprising calculus of the Christian life is that dying to self is the only way to truly live. It's counterintuitive, but you know it's true. Think of your happiest days, when all seemed right with the world and you were most thankful to be alive. Weren't they days in which you denied yourself and served someone else? Perhaps you remodeled a home for a handicapped person, babysat for a young couple who desperately needed a date, or flew across the country to surprise a friend.

Those days were your best because they beat with the dying-rising rhythm of the Christian life. As Good Friday leads to Easter morning, you died with Christ and discovered you were never more alive. Life with Christ begins now, carries on through your eventual death, and bursts in glory on the day of your resurrection.

Hear the paradox of the gospel: the one who desperately clutches at life inevitably strangles the life right out of his life. His struggle to survive is the very thing that kills him. But the one who denies himself for Jesus' sake, giving his best so others might flourish, finds that losing his life is precisely the way he finds it. Dying with Christ is not merely the *path* to life; it *is* life, now and forever.

Questions for Reflection

1. Why is sudden death a terrible way to go?

2. What do you think will make you perfectly happy and content?

3. How is dying to self the best way to prepare for your physical death? How is dying to self the best way to live now?

4. What are your idols? What are you doing to smash them?

SIXTEEN

HOPE

Those who hope in the Lord will renew their strength.

Isaiah 40:31

FOUR PHYSICALLY FIT ATHLETES were quickly losing their minds. Nick Schuyler, his best friend Will Bleakley, and their NFL friends Corey Smith and Marquis Cooper had gone out for a day of fishing on Marquis's boat. The boat flipped when they unwisely tried to free the anchor by attaching the line to the stern and gunning the motor, and now they were clinging to their capsized boat and praying for rescue.

Evening came and went with no sign of a search plane or boat. The frigid waves crested at more than seven feet, and the shivering friends spent the night falling off, climbing on, falling off, and climbing on the hull only to be swept off again. By morning Marquis was spent. Hypothermia and hopelessness scrambled his mind and he began to hallucinate. He vacillated between fierce acts of pointless aggression and the limp despair of a doomed man.

Soon Corey began to fade. He no longer tried to stay on the boat, but quietly held on as he floated in the water. About that time the men heard a helicopter overhead and saw its searchlight in the pounding surf, but it quickly flew by, taking their hope of rescue along with it. The men cursed and gave up. As Marquis died in Nick's arms, Corey let go of the boat, jerked his life jacket over his head, and slipped beneath the water.

Two days later, after Will had also succumbed to fatigue and despair, the Coast Guard found Nick, confused and barely alive, huddled on the stern of the overturned boat. Nick struggled with survivor's remorse. How did he make it through when his friends hadn't? He wrote a book to understand why and called it *Not Without Hope*.

Hope is the most underrated of all the Christian virtues. We know that the highest virtues are faith, hope, and love, but we focus on Paul's comment that "the greatest of these is love" and overlook the equally important fact that hope made the cut (1 Corinthians 13:13). We understand why faith is important, because we need something to believe, and why love is most important, because we need something to do. But how did hope, something to wait for, make it into the top tier?

> Hope is everything.

As Nick and his friends discovered, hope is everything. Hours after their boat capsized, Marquis and Corey were dead; it didn't take them long to lose their lives once they lost their hope. We can endure almost any crisis as long as we reasonably expect our situation to improve, but even common problems can devastate us if we have no hope of solving them.

To grasp the power of our Christian hope, consider how you would respond to the news that you have a serious illness. You would understandably be frightened and distraught, but you would also take comfort in your doctor's hope for a cure.

You would eagerly try any drug or procedure, no matter how experimental, if it offered a plausible path to recovery. But what if you had exhausted all options? What if there was nothing left to try and you had to go home and die? You could fall into despair, or you might realize that we're all terminal, so modern medicine is never more than a stop-gap measure. Your disease has burned a clearing through the underbrush of modern science, and with that out of the way, you can more plainly see the bedrock of your permanent Christian hope.

Our ultimate hope cannot be found *here* or *now*. It isn't *here*, for our finite world is limited in its ability to solve problems. We sometimes suppose that money and intelligence can fix anything—if we spend enough to hire the smartest minds, there are no obstacles we can't overcome. We secretly know that isn't true, for we all will die of something. We will eventually meet some problem that, because of our advancing age or lack of resources, will swamp our boats and take us out.

Our hope isn't *now*, for then it wouldn't be hope. Paul explains, "Hope that is seen is no hope at all. Who hopes for what he already has? But if we hope for what we do not yet have, we wait for it patiently" (Romans 8:24–25). Our hope isn't fulfilled now, for this present life won't last. The fleetingness of life led Paul to conclude, "if only for this life we have hope in Christ, we are to be pitied more than all men" (1 Corinthians 15:19).

Our hope isn't in the here and now but in the *there* and *then*. Our hope is not in anything down here but in the God who is up there. David writes, "Some trust in chariots and some in horses, but we trust in the name of the Lord our God. They are brought to their knees and fall, but we rise up and stand firm" (Psalm 20:7–8). Paul tells Timothy to "command those who are rich in this present world not to be arrogant nor to put their hope in wealth, which is so uncertain, but to put their hope in God" (1 Timothy 6:17).

Is anything less reliable—yet trusted more—than money? If we hide it under our mattresses and no thieves find it, still its value will be stolen by inflation. We may invest in stocks, bonds, and real estate, but these investments often drop like the temperature in January. In fear we may sink what is left of our money into a low-yield savings account, which is about the same as hiding it under our mattresses. If we can't protect the value of our money, how can we expect it to protect us?

Our only hope is to hope in God, who does not change with the whims of the economy or the diagnosis of our medical condition. Jeremiah fell into despair when Jerusalem was burned to the ground and all seemed lost, but from the barrenness of Babylon he remembered that God's "compassions never fail. They are new every morning; great is your faithfulness. I say to myself, 'The Lord is my portion; therefore I will wait for him" (Lamentations 3:21–24).

Our hope is in God—for what He is doing now but especially for what He will do *then*. God never said He would fix all of our problems now, but He has promised to "wipe every tear from [our] eyes" when he returns to make "everything new." Then "there will be no more death or mourning or crying or pain, for the old order of things has passed away" (Revelation 21:4–5). We have

> A resurrection only works in a cemetery.

God's promise for the future, so we can trust Him for whatever He brings our way today. Even when our backs are against the wall, we may respond with the gritty faith of Job, "Though he slay me, yet will I hope in him" (Job 13:15).

Our hope lies in what God will do in the future, and this future has broken into our present. The *there* and *then* entered the *here* and *now* when Jesus pumped His fist on Easter morning, for His resurrection was the sunrise of the first day of a whole new world. Jesus awoke the new creation as He broke the spell of sin and death. Death would continue to claim its victims, but no one who believes in Jesus need ever cower before death again. When the women came to the tomb to tend their Lord's body, they found it was death that had died in the night. They discovered that Jesus' love is stronger than death, and He, not death, will have the last word.

So we are never without hope. Not even when we're dead, and especially not then. Remember, a resurrection only works in a cemetery.

Questions for Reflection

1. Why is hope essential for life?

2. What are your hopes? How do these hopes motivate you? How do they help you to endure trials?

3. Have you learned that nothing in this life, such as money or talent, is worthy of your ultimate hope? What events helped you to learn this lesson?

4. Since resurrections only work in cemeteries, what does this mean for your impending death?

SEVENTEEN

HEAVEN

I desire to depart and be with Christ, which is
better by far.

Philippians 1:23

EVERYONE WANTS TO KNOW what happens when we die, and
they eagerly read books that promise to tell them. One such
book is Don Piper's description of what he saw and heard
during his *90 Minutes in Heaven*. This popular book spawned
two other bestsellers that tell the stories of boys who went to
heaven and returned: *The Boy Who Came Back from Heaven* and
*Heaven Is for Real: A Little Boy's Astounding Story of His Trip to
Heaven and Back*. It also inspired a book that went in the other
direction, *23 Minutes in Hell*. (Now we only need a Roman
Catholic book to complete the afterlife trifecta—perhaps
something with the title *7 Minutes in Purgatory*, which seemed
like forever, because, you know, it was purgatory.)

The firsthand accounts in these books have comforted and
challenged many, but rather than rely on the experience of
someone I haven't met, I will limit my comments on heaven to
what God reports in Scripture. Four passages tell us what happens to Christians the moment we die. In 2 Corinthians 5:6–9,

Paul wishes "to be away from the body and at home with the Lord," for, as he says in Philippians 1:21–24, when he dies he will "depart and be with Christ." Paul believes that all Christians who die go to be with Jesus, and he declares in 1 Thessalonians 4:14 that when Christ returns "God will bring with Jesus those who have fallen asleep in him." Paul's focus on Jesus reflects the words of his Lord, who told the thief on the cross, "Today you will be with me in paradise" (Luke 23:43).

These four texts all say the same thing: When we die, we go to be with Jesus. The passages say nothing more. Scripture does not elaborate further because this heavenly period—what theologians call the intermediate state between our death and resurrection—is not its focus. The Bible is much more interested in the end of the story, when we will return with Jesus for our resurrection bodies in order to live forever on the New Earth. As to the period of time before that return, when we are in heaven awaiting our resurrection, it is enough to know that we are with Jesus.

And that is enough, because Jesus is what makes heaven special. If heaven by itself is so much better than earth, Lazarus would have been annoyed when Jesus raised him from the dead. "Thanks for nothing," he would have said. "I was really enjoying heaven, and you brought me back here? How is that supposed to make me happy?!" Lazarus was glad to be resurrected because the first person he saw was Jesus, and His presence made Lazarus's tomb a literal heaven on earth. Likewise, Paul said he was eager to die, not so he could go to heaven, but so he could "be with Christ" (Philippians 1:23). Paul had been to heaven where he had probably seen Jesus. He knew what he was missing, and he longed to return and be reunited with his Lord (2 Corinthians 12:2–4).

Besides this indescribable joy of being with Jesus, we can't say much about what we will do in heaven. We won't have bodies, so it is hard to understand how we will do much except worship God and bask in the presence of Jesus—and even that is hard to comprehend, for we can't imagine doing anything without our bodies. Perhaps God will give us provisional bodies for this heavenly period, like a mechanic lends a loaner car while he is repairing ours. We just don't know.

We do have one other intriguing snapshot of heaven in Revelation 6:9–11. In John's vision, he sees martyred souls (clothed in white, so perhaps they have bodies of some type) calling out to God, "How long, Sovereign Lord, holy and true, until you judge the inhabitants of the earth and avenge our blood?" So it seems that one thing we will do in heaven is pray.

This is surprising, because we tend to think of heaven as a long vacation. Our work on earth is done, and we go to heaven for an eternal rest. Throughout history, many Christians have thought otherwise. The church father Origen wrote that "all those fathers who have fallen asleep before us fight on our side and aid us by their prayers." Gregory of Nazianzus declared at his father's funeral, "I am satisfied that he accomplishes there now by his prayers more than he ever did by his teaching." Thérèse of Lisieux said, "I wish to spend my heaven in doing good upon earth. . . . No, I shall not be able to take any rest until the end of the world."

> We may be dead, but we still belong to the communion of saints.

As an injured player continues to cheer his team from the sideline, so when we leave the contest on earth we will continue to support and pray for those who remain in the game. We will become part of the "great cloud of witnesses" that urges those still competing to "run with perseverance the race marked out for [them]" (Hebrews 12:1). We may be dead, but we still belong to the communion of saints.

Evangelical Christians don't tend to think much about the communion of saints. We say with the Apostles' Creed, "I believe in the communion of saints," and we sing in "The Church's One Foundation" that we have "mystic sweet communion with those whose rest is won," but most of us haven't stopped to consider what this means.

Briefly stated, the communion of saints is the belief that the entire company of saints, both in this life (the church militant) and the next (the church triumphant), is united in Jesus. We don't relate directly to those who have gone before, but we speak to Jesus about them and they speak to Jesus about us. We both remain in Jesus, and so the two branches of the church of God remain connected to each other. As Martin Luther wrote to his friend, "I shall pray for you, I ask that you pray for me. . . . If I depart this life ahead of you—something I desire—then I must pull you after me. If you depart before me, then you shall pull me after you. For we confess *one* God and with all saints we abide in our Savior."

Scripture describes this communion of saints in the thrilling words of Hebrews 12:22–24:

> But you have come to Mount Zion, to the heavenly Jerusalem, the city of the living God. You have come to thousands upon thousands of angels in joyful assembly, to the church of the firstborn, whose names are written in heaven. You have come to God, the judge of all men, to the spirits of righteous men made perfect, to Jesus the mediator of a new covenant, and to the sprinkled blood that speaks a better word than the blood of Abel.

Did you notice how the living saints ("you"), dead saints ("the heavenly Jerusalem"), and even the angels are united together in Jesus? The communion of saints is also present in that strange passage of Matthew 27:51–53. When Jesus died, "the earth shook and the rocks split," and "the tombs broke open and the bodies of many holy people who had died were raised to life. They came out of the tombs, and after Jesus' resurrection they went into the holy city and appeared to many people." Jesus' death and resurrection brought the church militant and the church triumphant together. It still does.

> Death may push us to the sideline, but we remain an important part of the game.

Death cannot separate us from the love of Christ or from each other in the body of Christ. Death moves us into the triumphant wing of the church, where we continue to have "mystic sweet communion" with those who are still fighting. We can't say what details we will know about individuals in the militant church, but we will pray for them and for Jesus' swift return. Death may push us to the sideline, but we remain an important part of the game.

Questions for Reflection

1. Why does Scripture not offer many details about heaven?

2. What person(s) do you most want to see when you get to heaven?

3. What do you think you will do in heaven? How can you best prepare for that now?

4. How does the biblical teaching of the communion of saints encourage you?

EIGHTEEN

EARTH

He who was seated on the throne said, "I am
making everything new!"

Revelation 21:5

I PREACHED MY GRANDMOTHER'S funeral by viewing her life
through the lens of the biblical story of creation, fall, and
redemption. I began with creation, explaining that God made
Grandma in His image and placed her on earth to flourish
and thrive. And did she ever. Grandma squeezed every last
drop out of life, much like the discarded orange rinds from
her homemade juice. She had spunk.

Grandma went parasailing on her seventieth birthday. She
sang solos in her church Christmas cantata long after the use-
by date on her voice had expired. She drove a muscle car, a
1972 Chevelle Malibu, making her the only eighty-year-old
woman to draw stares from young men as she drove down
the street. Her daughter told her to place a "Not for Sale"
sign in the back window to fend off their advances, but when
one unfortunate fellow followed her anyway, my annoyed
grandma pulled over, got out of her car, and approached the
young man.

"Why are you following me?" she demanded. He stammered that he wondered if she'd like to sell her car.

She thrust her finger at the sign and said, "Do you see my sign? It says, 'Not for sale.' Can't you read?"

"I guess not," the man said.

"No, I should say not," she harrumphed, and drove off.

Grandma loved to tease. She often told me that my children are cute, so they must take after their mother. When I told her this fact also reflected poorly on her, she cackled with the delight of being caught and tried another line of attack. Her mind stayed sharp until the end, in part because of her daily walks and time with young people. How many eighty-year-olds do you know who are the toast of their church youth group?

Grandma often seemed to look for trouble. When I was five years old, she took me to McDonald's, and we sat in her Chevelle and each finished off a cheeseburger and fries. She asked if I wanted dessert. I didn't usually get dessert in restaurants, so I said yes, I'd like an apple pie. After I ate that, she asked if I was still hungry. I said sure, I could go for another burger. For the next hour she kept feeding me quarters, sending me back in for more fries, burgers, and apple pies. Each time was funnier than the last because we couldn't believe how much food we were putting away. She couldn't wait to drive me home, where she proudly announced to my surprised parents how she had tempted me into the sin of gluttony and had elevated my expectations for the next time they took me to McDonald's. It may be a coincidence, but I was never left alone with Grandma in a restaurant after that.

After this reflection on Grandma's zest for life, I told the mourners how her life had been broken by the fall. Grandma was a sinner. She was opinionated and a bit stubborn, and sometimes her strong personality rubbed people the wrong way.

She also suffered much from the sin of others. Five years into her marriage, her husband walked out on her and their family, leaving her to care as best she could for their two children. But she had help. I thanked Abe and Mary Yoder, who stepped into the void left by my grandfather and became parent figures to my father and his sister. Abe and Mary welcomed them into their home and took them on vacations. Abe became the father they never had.

Scripture says the sins of fathers are passed on to the third and fourth generations, but Abe and Mary broke the cycle. Thanks in large part to their love, my dad was the polar opposite of his father, and my brothers and I grew up in a nurturing, loving home. We and our children are part of Abe and Mary's legacy.

I mentioned that the most obvious consequence of the fall was what brought us there that day. Grandma's death reminds us that we live in a broken world. Grandma died—and we all will die—because of sin. We weep for our loss, and the worst part is knowing that we can do nothing about it.

But that doesn't mean nothing has been done about it. I moved on to the most thrilling stretch of God's story, His final act of redemption. I explained that God does not make junk, for creation is good. And He is not about to junk what He has made—He will redeem His world. The empire will strike back; the curse will be reversed.

> Those who die in Christ are on the first leg of a journey that is round-trip.

The good news of the gospel is that Grandma's life on earth has been interrupted, but only temporarily. Death has unnaturally broken her in two. Her corpse remains here, but her soul is already with Jesus in heaven. We are comforted beyond words to know her soul is with Jesus, but that is not the end of her story. The Christian hope is that Grandma is on the first leg of a journey that is round-trip. Someday soon she will return with her Lord to this planet. Jesus will resurrect her body, put her back together, and she will live forever with Jesus as a whole person, here, on our restored earth.

The earthiness of our resurrection hope surprises many believers, but it is repeatedly taught throughout Scripture. God announced, "I will create new heavens and a new earth" (Isaiah 65:17). Peter said, "We are looking forward to a new heaven and a new earth" (2 Peter 3:13). John reports that his final vision began with "a new heaven and a new earth" (Revelation 21:1).

What will be new about the New Earth? The fall and its curse will be removed. Peter declares that unlike our sinful age, the New Earth will be "the home of righteousness" (2 Peter 3:13). What will be the same about the New Earth? It will still be the earth. God declares, "I am making everything new," not "I am making new everything" (Revelation 21:5). God will not create new things, but He will redeem the things He created.

> God will not create new things, but He will redeem the things He created.

Redemption restores rather than obliterates creation. God will not blow up this world and start over someplace else, for that would concede that Satan has so corrupted His world even God can't get it back. Satan must win nothing in the end; everything sin broke, grace will restore.

The New Earth must be similar to this one, for just as "future you" must be really you to count as your resurrection, so the New Earth must still be the earth to count as its redemption. If the New Earth is too different from the present earth, the earth wouldn't be *redeemed* but *replaced*. Since redemption restores creation, we can expect those things pronounced good at creation to make it through to the New Earth, while the fall and its corrosive effects are removed. The Great Lakes, Mount Everest, and every species of animal may well be there, for the New Earth is this earth, freed from the damage of sin.

What will we do on this New Earth? Probably many of the same things we do now, but without the handicap of sin. We will be fully human and fully alive, and we will have forever to do what we were made to do. We will join our hearts to worship God, but we will also love and serve each other, and try our hand at various forms of culture. Isaiah declares that God will be the glory of the New Earth, yet we will continue to "build houses and dwell in them . . . plant vineyards and eat their fruit" (Isaiah 60:1–3; 65:21). Personally, I'm looking forward to eating more of Grandma's homemade mashed potatoes, fudge, and whoopie pies.

If you have repented of your sins and daily strive to submit to Jesus' reign in your life, then you will join my grandmother in her resurrection. You will live forever on a restored earth, free from sin and its devastation. No more cross words, wounded spirits, disease, or death.

Come quickly, Lord Jesus.

Questions for Reflection

1. How has your life been broken by the fall?

2. If you had thirty seconds to explain the Christian hope, what would you say?

3. We can't take anything with us when we leave this earth. But given that we will return with Jesus, what things might you come back to?

4. What excites you most about the biblical vision of the New Earth? Why is this hope even better than heaven, and the exact opposite of hell?

NINETEEN

MORE

Now the dwelling of God is with men, and he will live with them.

Revelation 21:3

STAR PITCHER STEPHEN STRASBURG grimaced as he released the ball. He stared at his right arm and shook it, but he couldn't shake the pain throbbing in his elbow. One awkward pitch had torn his ulnar collateral ligament, ending his phenomenal rookie season and making him a candidate for Tommy John surgery.

That's not all bad. The surgery, first performed on Dodger pitcher Tommy John in 1974, replaces the torn ligament in the elbow with a tendon from the forearm, hamstring, or foot. Pitchers require more than a year of grueling rehabilitation to recover from the surgery, but many come back throwing harder than ever. The procedure is so successful that some pitchers who aren't even injured look into having it done. Tommy John surgery appears to do the impossible; it rescues the careers of shattered pitchers and makes their arms better than new. This surgery anticipates medically what God will do cosmically, for it does for one pitcher what God will do for the entire world.

Last chapter summarized the biblical story of creation, fall, and redemption, but what I didn't say then was that the final act of redemption also includes a consummation. God will not merely restore creation to its original goodness. He will consummate it, taking our world to that higher place it was always intended to go. Our end on the New Earth will far surpass our beginning in Eden, in at least five ways.

First and foremost, God will live here permanently. In the garden of Eden, God intermittently walked with Adam and Eve. He came and left, came and left, but in the end He will come here to stay. Listen to the thrilling conclusion of Scripture: "And I heard a loud voice from the throne saying, 'Now the dwelling of God is with men, and he will live with them. They will be his people, and God himself will be with them and be their God'" (Revelation 21:3).

Three times in this verse God declares He will live with us. He wants us to be so sure of his coming that he calls himself Immanuel, which means "God with us" (Matthew 1:23). Most of my life I read that name backward, thinking it meant "us with God" and that the Christian hope was to go to heaven and live with God. While that would be a wonderful privilege, it's an even greater honor for God to come live with us.

The story of Scripture is the story of Immanuel, for every time God appears in Scripture He stays here a little longer and in a little more permanent form. He comes and goes from the garden of Eden. Then he's the pillar and cloud leading the exodus. Next He appears as Jesus—God in tangible, physical flesh. Now He is present invisibly and within us by His Holy Spirit. Finally—can you believe it?—He descends to earth to live with us forever. How committed is God to us and to our world? He loves us so much that He permanently became one of us (Jesus will always be fully God and fully man) and He will permanently reside here with us. Scripture ends with

God descending to dwell with us. Heaven, the abode of God, literally comes to earth.

Second, the God who comes to "wipe every tear from their eyes" will also eliminate the source of those tears (Revelation 21:4). Unlike Adam and Eve, who were created good but with the potential to sin, on the New Earth we will have the absolute certainty that the God who restored our goodness will not allow us to fall away again. Augustine explained how our end is better than our beginning by playfully noting that Adam and Eve were *able not to sin*, while in glory we will *not be able to sin*. Imagine how good life will be on the New Earth: We will live forever in loving community with God and each other, with the peace of mind that comes from knowing we will never mess this up.

> Heaven, the abode of God, literally comes to earth.

Third, we will live together in our resurrection, "spiritual" bodies (1 Corinthians 15:42–49). These spiritual bodies will still be material, for they are patterned after Jesus' resurrection body, and Jesus after His resurrection pointedly ate fish and invited His friends to touch Him. "Look at my hands and my feet," our resurrected Lord told His disciples. "It is I myself! Touch me and see; a ghost does not have flesh and bones, as you see I have" (Luke 24:39). If Jesus is "the first-fruits" of our resurrection, then we can expect our resurrection bodies to be as physical as His (1 Corinthians 15:20).

Our spiritual bodies won't be less than physical, but they will be more. Our spiritual bodies will be animated by the "life-giving spirit" of "the last Adam," so that they will be unable to die (1 Corinthians 15:45). Unlike our present bodies, which begin to break down if we go a few days without food and water, our resurrection bodies will be guaranteed to live forever (which is why I'm saving hang gliding for the New Earth).

Fourth, we will use our resurrection bodies to enjoy forever our escalating human culture. Jesus will not return with a giant eraser to wipe out the accomplishments of history. He will not send us back to Eden to start over from scratch, but we will enter the New Earth with whatever level of human culture we have achieved. The story of Scripture begins in a garden and ends in a city, the New Jerusalem. The progress from garden to city suggests that God never intended for us to remain in a state of pure nature but to take the raw materials of creation and develop the best of human culture.

If you enjoy the good life, imagine a world where artists such as Bach and Michelangelo have forever to write music, sculpt, and paint—all without the handicap of sin. If you like being human and you like living here, you are going to love life on the New Earth.

> If you like being human and you like living here, you are going to love life on the New Earth.

Fifth, there is one benefit of the consummation that is better not *despite* our fall but precisely *because* of it. Adam and Eve knew that God was good, but they could never have guessed the depth of His love until they had rebelled and been restored. Forgiven sinners like us understand the grace of God even better than the angels, who stand on tiptoe to peer into the gospel, trying to make sense of it (1 Peter 1:12). Because they have never needed the grace of salvation, the unfallen angels can only puzzle at the patient mercy of God that we know by experience.

In at least these five ways, the consummation is "redemption plus." The end exceeds the beginning, for God created His world to continually grow and develop. Creation will never max out but will be "brought into the glorious freedom of the children of God" (Romans 8:21). All who have repented of their deadly sin and longed for Jesus' coming will live forever with Him here, on a restored earth. We will flourish in every aspect of human life, enjoying laughter and companionship as together we worship the God whose holy and loving nature will always exceed our grasp.

As I write this, the sports world is waiting for Stephen Strasburg to begin his rehabilitation program. He will start to throw off the mound in a few weeks, and then pitch a few innings in games. His team hopes to have him back by the end of summer. Will he be better than ever? We'll have to wait and see. Jesus will soon return to this earth, maybe by the end of summer, and when He comes He will repair our world so it is better than ever. Just you wait and see.

Questions for Reflection

1. Why is it difficult to imagine how life will be on the New Earth?

2. What tears will God need to wipe from your eyes? (See Revelation 21:4.)

3. Why is Jesus the center of the New Earth? Why is it important to say that we will do more than sing worship songs to him forever?

4. What most amazes you about grace? Do you think you will ever comprehend this?

TWENTY

LAMENT

What I feared has come upon me; what I dreaded has happened to me. I have no peace, no quietness; I have no rest, but only turmoil.

Job 3:25–26

THE FIRST HALF OF this book scouted death, our last enemy. We examined its causes, consequences, and the psychological warfare it inflicts upon every member of the human race. The second half explored Jesus' victory over death—how His cross and resurrection conquered death, how we join His triumph through faith and repentance, and what His victory secures for us in heaven and on the New Earth. With this big picture in view, I now close with three chapters of practical advice for those who are nearing the end of their lives. If you are dying in Christ, you must learn to *lament*, *live*, and when the time comes, be prepared to *let go*.

When John Piper was diagnosed with prostate cancer, he practiced what he had long preached and sought comfort in his sovereign God. On the eve of what turned out to be his entirely successful surgery, Piper shared his top ten lessons in a blog post entitled, "Don't Waste Your Cancer." The first two lessons are vintage Piper: "You will waste your cancer if you do not believe it is designed for you by God," and "You will waste your cancer if you believe it is a curse and not a gift."

Piper may be overselling—is cancer really God's gift designed for you?—but his emphasis on God's sovereignty is well taken. It may be hard to imagine that evil comes from the hand of God, but it's even worse to think it doesn't. On the day Job lost his wealth and dear children, he responded, "The Lord gave and the Lord has taken away; may the name of the Lord be praised" (Job 1:21). When his wife told him to "curse God and die," Job replied, "You are talking like a foolish woman. Shall we accept good from God, and not trouble?" (2:9–10). God agreed with Job's assessment, and the inspired narrator concludes the story by saying that Job's siblings "comforted and consoled him over all the trouble the Lord had brought upon him" (42:11).

The sovereignty of God puts the *problem* in the problem of evil. We can't understand why an all-powerful and all-loving God would allow His children to suffer so much. Job can only conclude, though he trembles to say it, that God has wronged him (19:6). He complains that "the arrows of the Almighty are in me, my spirit drinks in their poison" (6:4). He continues, "If I have sinned, what have I done to you, O watcher of men? Why have you made me your target?" (7:20).

But the sovereignty of God is more than a problem. It is our only refuge when trouble comes, for the moment our lives begin falling apart is precisely the time we need to know that our gracious God is keeping it all together. We would not bother to cry out to God unless we believed He loves us enough to care and is strong enough to answer our prayer.

As the Heidelberg Catechism memorably declares, my only comfort is knowing "that I am not my own, but belong—

body and soul, in life and in death—to my faithful Savior Jesus Christ. He has fully paid for all my sins with his precious blood, and has set me free from the tyranny of the devil. He also watches over me in such a way that not a hair can fall from my head without the will of my Father in heaven: in fact, all things must work together for my salvation."

> Nothing comforts a troubled soul like the sovereignty of God.

Nothing comforts a troubled soul like the sovereignty of God, and nothing else invites us to pour out our hearts to Him. Some people mistakenly suppose that God's sovereignty requires pious passivity, and they share prayer requests that go something like this: "My husband is out of work, and I just learned that I have cancer and will need to start chemotherapy next week. Please pray that I will remain open to whatever God wants to teach me."

I appreciate how this person is choosing to trust God, but I wonder if she is being honest with her feelings and with God. Job responded much more aggressively: "I cry out to you, O God, but you do not answer . . . You turn on me ruthlessly; with the might of your hand you attack me" (30:20–21). And yet God concluded that Job spoke better than his three friends, who counseled him to confess he deserved whatever came his way (42:7).

I also wonder how this person will know when she has learned God's lesson. Moses explained that "the secret things belong to the Lord our God, but the things revealed belong to us and to our children forever" (Deuteronomy 29:29). God has not promised to tell us why this layoff or that disease happened to us, but He has revealed that we should expect such things in a fallen world. We hate the fall, and so we detest and mourn every loss it produces.

The fall and God's sovereignty should combine to prompt this sort of prayer request: "I'm sad and scared and fumbling around in the dark. I can't eat, I can't sleep, and I have to remind myself to breathe. I need you to cry with me, to share in my grief. I don't think I can make it on my own. So please pray with me. Pray that I will feel God's love and have the strength to trust Him for what I need each day."

Counselor Dave Powlison was diagnosed with prostate cancer shortly after his friend John Piper, and with Piper's permission he inserted his own reflections into Piper's ten ways to not waste your cancer. While affirming Piper's robust view of God's sovereignty, Powlison equally emphasized the fallenness of cancer. Where Piper said cancer is a gift rather than a curse, Powlison pointed out that cancer itself is evil, though our loving Father "works a most kind good through our most grievous losses." Where Piper declared that cancer "is designed for you by God," Powlison added, "Recognizing his designing hand does not make you stoic or dishonest or artificially buoyant. Instead, the reality of God's design elicits and channels your honest outcry to your one true Savior. God's design invites honest speech, rather than silencing us into resignation."

Powlison balanced the fall with God's sovereignty and declared that belief in both should lead to more lament rather than less. If you think about it, those who don't believe in both a fall and a sovereign God have no right to mourn. If there is no fall, then nothing is really wrong. If there is no God, then nothing can be done about it anyway.

But we who believe in a sovereign God feel the fall deep in our bones. Powlison explained, "In Christ, you know what's at stake, and so you keenly feel the wrong of this fallen world. You don't take pain and death for granted." We know this world is not the way it's supposed to be, and we know that God possesses the power and love to set things right. So we cry out for God to pity us and change our plight. If we ever stop lamenting, it can only mean we've given up.

We presently live in the tension between the fall and the sovereignty of God. The fall means our world is broken by sin and death, while God's sovereignty assures us that He remains in charge and will restore all things at our resurrection. We grieve, but not as those without hope. We hope, but not as those who do not grieve.

> We grieve, but not as those without hope. We hope, but not as those who do not grieve.

We may not understand why this or that is happening to us, but we know that any suffering is an opportunity to declare our allegiance. We refuse to curse God and die; instead we choose the tenacious faith of Job: "He knows the way that I take; when he has tested me, I will come forth as gold" (Job 23:10).

Questions for Reflection

1. Why is God your only comfort when facing death?

2. Are you honestly admitting your fears and sorrows? Why is it important to tell God exactly what you are feeling?

3. What happens to the hearts of people who refuse to lament? Do you think God is pleased with them?

4. How might pouring out your grief and anguish to God actually be a sign of great faith?

TWENTY-ONE

LIVE

Always give yourselves fully to the work of the Lord, because you know that your labor in the Lord is not in vain.

1 Corinthians 15:58

CHAPTER 2 OPENED WITH the story of Matt Chandler, the dynamic young pastor who suffered a brain seizure on Thanksgiving morning. Because the life expectancy for his stage 3 tumor is two to three years, Matt lives each day as if it were his last. "It's *carpe diem* on steroids," he said as he constructed a peanut butter and jelly sandwich right after another father-son trip to the park. More than most dads his age, Matt relishes noisy dinners, baby burpings, diaper changings, and enthusiastic rounds of "Twinkle, Twinkle, Little Star."

Most people understand why. Scarcity creates value, and Matt's days become more precious as they become fewer. So he milks each moment, cuddling with his children at story time, lingering ten minutes too long as he tucks them into bed, and squeezing their tiny hands as if he'll never have to let go.

Most people think they understand why, but they are wrong. Matt's heightened sense of reality cannot be explained solely by his dwindling supply of days. If death extinguishes our existence, then ultimately it doesn't matter if we invest our remaining days in our children or squander them in front of the television. The father of the year dies, as does the deadbeat dad, so if this life is all there is, we might as well be the latter. Paul explained, "If the dead are not raised, 'Let us eat and drink, for tomorrow we die'" (1 Corinthians 15:32).

Matt's passion for life is not a desperate attempt to cling to what he will inevitably lose, but it arises from his belief in the resurrection. Matt savors his remaining moments with his family precisely because he plans on seeing them again. If he leads his children to Jesus, Matt knows he will live with them forever. What a payoff!

Some authors suggest that Christians who hope for the afterlife cheapen the value of this life. They claim that if we know we will live forever, then we won't be too interested in our present life. We won't worry about loving our neighbor or righting wrongs, but we will let things slide as we coast into glory.

The apostle Paul says that just the opposite is true, for our hope in the afterlife is the very thing that gives meaning to life now. After expounding the glorious truth of the resurrection for fifty-seven verses, Paul concludes 1 Corinthians 15 by applying our future hope to the present: "Therefore, my dear brothers, stand firm. Let nothing move you. Always give yourselves fully to the work of the Lord, because you know that your labor in the Lord is not in vain" (v. 58).

The resurrection empowers us to *stand firm*. We plant ourselves in the soil of the gospel, throwing down deep roots in the promise that we will live again. Our lives may bend in the hurricane winds of tumor and tragedy, but roots that have wrapped themselves around the bedrock of God's promise keep us firmly grounded in the gospel. Our God has defeated death, so we need not be moved, or even overly impressed, by any storm that may break upon us.

The resurrection frees us to *give ourselves fully to the work of the Lord*. We don't merely assume a defensive posture, gritting our teeth in the face of gale-force winds, but our hope in the resurrection inspires us to do our best work for the Lord. We know that our labor is not in vain, for Jesus will return to resurrect and reward us for what we have done. "Whatever you do," writes Paul, "work at it with all your heart, as working for the Lord, not for men, since you know that you will receive an inheritance from the Lord as a reward" (Colossians 3:23–24).

> Our God has defeated death, so we need not be moved by any storm that may break upon us.

The resurrection means there is continuity between this life and the next. Jesus will return to restore our world, and He will use our scraps of "gold, silver, [and] costly stones" in its construction (1 Corinthians 3:12). Like a master artist who fashions a painting from the rough drawing of his apprentice, adding depth and splashes of color to his student's sketched lines, Jesus will enfold our squiggles into the final portrait of His redeemed creation.

So we put our heart into whatever is before us. If we are parents, we patiently discipline our children as if eternity is at stake. If we are a maid or mechanic, we clean rooms and fix cars as if they were our own. If we are students, we strive to master the material, knowing that someday someone may depend on us for what we have learned. If we are rich, we follow Paul's command that those with wealth should "put their hope in God" and commit "to do good, to be rich in good deeds, and to be generous and willing to share. In this way they will lay up treasure for themselves as a firm foundation for the coming age, so that they may take hold of the life that is truly life" (1 Timothy 6:17–19).

We take hold of life when we work for the Lord by giving ourselves to others. Because the Lord's work stands forever, we know that our "labor in the Lord is not in vain" (1 Corinthians 15:58). Our works may pass away when we do, but they will rise with us to be rewarded in the next life.

But what if you have come to the end of your life and you no longer have the strength to work for the Lord? Dr. Martin Lloyd-Jones was one of the great preachers of the twentieth century, but by 1981 he was bedridden and unable to study and preach as he once had. His biographer and friend Ian Murray asked if it was difficult for him to be "on the shelf." Lloyd-Jones replied with Jesus' words, "Do not rejoice that the spirits submit to you, but rejoice that your names are written in heaven" (Luke 10:20). He said that he was perfectly content, for his name was written in heaven. How could he possibly be more blessed?

Lloyd-Jones knew the surprising secret of the gospel: ultimate satisfaction does not come from what we do for Jesus but from resting in what Jesus has done for us. We are fulfilled the moment we put our faith in Christ. Everything else is gravy. Of course, when we understand what Jesus has done for us—giving His life so we might live—we will cherish our lives now.

Debbie Middlemann told this story about her mother, Edith, the ninety-four-year-old widow of Francis Schaeffer. Francis wrote powerfully about the dangers of euthanasia and the gift of life, and now his wife and daughter were putting his beliefs into practice. Debbie said that Swiss hospices slowly euthanize their patients, giving them ever increasing amounts of morphine to hasten their exit. But Debbie would have none of it. She brought her mother home and insisted that she savor the life that was left by eating home-cooked meals and listening to her favorite albums and books.

When Edith observes that she's old and may not live much longer, Debbie reminds her that she has what any young person has—this day. None of us know if we will be alive tomorrow, but we do know God has given us this day. What will we do with it? We can choose to give up and wait to die, or we can anticipate our glorious future by defiantly stomping on the face of death. We choose life.

> God has given us this day. What will we do with it?
>
> ⸺∞⸺

Questions for Reflection

1. Meditate on 1 Corinthians 15:32, "If the dead are not raised, 'Let us eat and drink, for tomorrow we die.'" Why is the resurrection of Jesus necessary for our lives to have meaning?

2. How does our hope for the next life provide the only incentive to enjoy and work hard in this one?

3. If the resurrection inspires enthusiastic effort, then what does laziness imply about our hope?

4. What efforts of yours might Jesus include in his restoration of creation?

TWENTY-TWO

LET GO

Lord Jesus, receive my spirit.

Acts 7:59

D. A. CARSON TELLS the story of nearly three hundred friends who gathered for a Saturday prayer service to implore God to heal their friend Mary, a beloved Christian who was dying of breast cancer. As the day wore on, their prayers became more intense. "Lord, you say where two or three are gathered, you will hear their prayer," said one, "and we've got two hundred eighty-four!" Another said that faith as small as a mustard seed was all it took to receive what they asked, and they certainly had that. Another claimed God's healing by reminding Jesus that He is the Great Physician. He had healed people in the past, and since He is the same yesterday, today, and forever, He should perform a miracle on their friend now.

One participant, herself a cancer survivor, had heard enough of these mighty prayer warriors telling God what He must do. When it came her turn, she prayed, "Lord, we'd be so grateful if you would heal our friend Mary. But if not, teach her to die well. May she face the end of her life with gratitude, growing each day in holiness and leaving a legacy for her family and those who love her. Prepare her to meet her Maker. Teach her to die well."

The others gasped at this quitter in their midst, but later Mary's husband confided that it was exactly what he and his wife needed to hear. Their well-intentioned friends had unwittingly formed a conspiracy of healing. They had repeatedly assured them that God would heal Mary, so on top of the burden of breast cancer, Mary struggled with the spiritual pressure to get well. Consequently, she felt she would let everyone down if her condition worsened or even if she had a bad day. What a relief to learn she could let go!

> Letting go requires more faith than trusting God for a miracle.

Letting go requires more faith than trusting God for a miracle. If faith is our response to the Word of God, then we have faith only when we claim one of God's promises. God has not promised that we will recover—even those who presume God's healing eventually die from something—but He does guarantee we will rise again. So it isn't faith to boss God or attempt to guilt Him into keeping a promise He never made. Those who demand a miracle actually show they lack faith, for they are so afraid of dying that they are willing to order God around just to prolong their lives.

We should use modern medicine as God's weapon to help us fight for life. But when normal measures are exhausted, we demonstrate true faith by conceding that we don't have to get better now. We rest in God's promise that we will rise again, and we trust Him enough to die.

My friend Jeff stopped by the hospital to visit one of his dearest senior saints. Charlotte was in her eighties, but she had been young enough in heart to blossom under Jeff's ministry. She had paid close attention as Jeff proclaimed the story of God—how the world began with God's good creation, suffered a cataclysmic fall that ruined us and everything else, is being redeemed by Jesus' cross and resurrection, and will be consummated when Jesus returns and delivers this world to His Father.

Charlotte said learning God's story had changed her life. "I get it now," she told anyone who would listen. "The parts of the Bible make sense when you read them in light of the whole. For the first time in my life, I understand how my salvation fits into the larger picture."

> We rest in God's promise that we will rise again, and we trust Him enough to die.

Now Charlotte was dying. She chatted with her pastor about family, church, and the general quality of hospital food, and then Jeff said a prayer and promised to come see her again.

Jeff was minutes from home when his cell phone rang. It was the floor nurse calling from the hospital.

"Charlotte told me to contact you," she began. "She said that it's time for her to die. She told me to tell you not to hurry; she'll wait until you get here."

Jeff turned his car around and drove slightly faster than Charlotte had recommended. He feared she would die before he returned, and he prayed God would grant her sufficient stamina to hold on. He need not have worried. When he entered her room, panting from his swift jog from the parking garage, Charlotte called him over to her bed. She took his hand, looked into his eyes, and said, "Pastor, tell me the story one more time."

For the next twenty minutes, with a heavy but grateful heart, Jeff reviewed the story that had saved their lives. He told Charlotte about their gracious, triune God who created our world from love and for His glory. He reminded her that God put us here as His "image bearers" to take care of this world on His behalf (see Genesis 1:26–28). God intended us to flourish in all of our relationships—with Him, one another, and creation—and we would as long as we rested in His care and obeyed His loving will.

Jeff then described the destruction of the fall and how our rebellion against the one, true, and living God had shattered everything we were meant to be. We rejected God's love, fought with each other, and brought a curse upon the entire creation. We were doomed, unwilling and unable to take the first step toward reconciliation. We were "without hope and without God in the world" (Ephesians 2:12).

Jeff and Charlotte remembered how God refused to let the world end this way, and He sent His Son to rescue us from sin and death. Jesus offered His sinless life in our place, absorbing the wrath of God that we deserved so we could be adopted as the righteous children of God. Our loving Lord was crucified, dead, and buried, but three days later He shocked the world by rising from the dead.

Jesus ascended to heaven where He rules the world and intercedes for us before our merciful Father. He will soon return to make all things new. He will restore our humanity, repairing our relationships with God, each other, and creation. And He will bring joy to the world, far as the curse is found, by abolishing sin, disease, and death. No more tearful goodbyes! Because Jesus lives, we too shall live—with Him, here, glorifying God and enjoying Him forever!

Jeff's voice cracked and Charlotte's eyes filled with tears. "It's true," she whispered. "I know it's true." She smiled, and then cleared her throat and asked, "Pastor, will you call for the nurse?"

When the nurse entered the room, Charlotte said with resolute voice, "Nurse, I'd like a clean robe and I'd like my teeth." She turned to Jeff and patted his arm, "It's time. It's going to be okay."

Jeff left the room while the nurse dressed Charlotte in a white robe and put her teeth in, and when she was ready, Jeff returned, took her hand, and kissed her on the forehead. As Jeff prayed beside her, Charlotte raised her eyes toward heaven, and with a serenity that comes from knowing how the story ends, she repeated the words "thank you, thank you, thank you." By the third "thank you" she had fallen asleep, and on the fourth she was waking up in heaven.

Questions for Reflection

1. Why is it a lack of faith to demand that God heal us?

2. Why is it a lack of faith to expect that He won't?

3. How will you know when it is time to let go?

4. Are you entirely alone as you let go and fall into the hands of God? Who walks with you through the valley of the shadow of death?

TWENTY-THREE

FINISH WELL

I have fought the good fight, I have finished the
race, I have kept the faith.

2 Timothy 4:7

MARTIN LUTHER'S DEATH WAS closely watched by both
Roman Catholics and Protestants. Catholics had long sug-
gested that Luther was the son of Satan, so they expected
him to die a miserable and despairing death, racked with the
panic and pain of cardiac arrest as the devil drug him down
to hell. Protestants honored Luther as the hero of the Refor-
mation, and they hoped he would die with the same confident conviction that had carried him through life.

The decisive moment arrived a few hours after midnight
on February 18, 1546. As Luther lay dying in a bed far from
home, a nearby pastor was called to hear his last confession.
Justin Jonas roused him and asked, "Reverend father, will you
die steadfast in Christ and the doctrines you have preached?"

"Yes," replied Luther in a clear, calm voice. He fell back
asleep, this time for good. Later that morning an artist came
to paint a portrait of the dead man's peaceful face. Luther's
opponents might spread lies about his tortured soul, but his

followers would have the assurance that the faith that had supported Luther in death was sufficient to sustain them in life.

Luther's serene passing is a reminder that we never die alone. Many people watch as we die—some we know and some we don't—searching for signs that our faith is true. Death is the final and ultimate test. Life surprises us with pop quizzes and even a few midterms as we face the death of dreams, marriages, and careers. How we respond to these challenges may help us gauge how we will score on our final exam, but we will never know for sure until we sit for it.

> Many people watch as we die, searching for signs that our faith is true.

Everyone knows they must take this test, and they hunt anxiously for answers to help them prepare. They find little help in the world at large, for most people who manage to die in peace do so either by cutting off their head or ripping out their heart.

The "Sappy Leapers" suppress their minds and follow their hearts, which want to believe that somehow the next life will be even better than this one. They don't have any reason to think this is true, they just do. An example is Willie Nelson, who may have been smoking his prized marijuana when he gave this answer to a question on death: "Death is not the end of anything. I believe all of us are only energy that becomes matter. When the matter goes away, the energy still exists. You can't destroy it. It never dies. It manifests itself somewhere else. We are never alone. Even by ourselves, we are not alone. Death is just a door opening to somewhere else. Someday we'll know what that door opens to. I believe that. I really do." Nelson seems to be creating his beliefs on the fly, and saying he *really* believes what he is making up indicates he probably knows it isn't true.

The "Stoic Losers" work the problem from the other direction. They stuff their emotions and face death with a stiff upper lip that grudgingly accepts their fate. Their heads realize that they can't do anything to prolong their lives. The game is over and they are going away. The only thing left to them is to make a virtue out of being vanquished, so they ignore their anguish and blankly sigh, "We had a good run, didn't we? Hold on to the memories!" Their tough façade may seem admirable, but nothing changes the fact that they and their memory are slipping away faster than sand through the fingers of time.

We avoid these dead ends when we keep both our heads and our hearts. Christians sacrifice neither, for with heads grounded in the truth of God's Word, our hearts deeply feel both the agony of death and the joyful shout of resurrection. We know we must pass through death to live forever, for our resurrection does not eliminate death but follows it. Our resurrection does not replace death; it's what we find when we come out the other side. So we lament the carnage of the fall, but living in the promise of our redemption, we let go and fall forward into the strong arms of our loving Father.

Few people want to die, but there are two advantages to knowing your time is short. First, if you are a follower of Jesus, an imminent death means you are close to persevering in your faith. Perseverance is the goal of every Christian, for it means we have finished our race and are safely home with God. Some people walk with God for decades and then toss their faith aside in a midlife crisis. They didn't persevere. Others were saved for only a few days before they died. Though their Christian career was much shorter, they persevered until the end. Ultimately it doesn't matter how far you ran but whether you finished. Should you ever learn you have only a few months to live, among everything else it means that God has graciously moved you ahead of the other runners. You can see the finish line from where you stand, so sprint to the tape.

Second, when you know you are dying, you have the blessing of time to prepare. At the beginning of his career, as he was fending off attacks from prince and pope, a harried Martin Luther made time to answer a persistent man's questions about death. In "A Sermon on Preparing to Die," Luther said the best way to prepare for death is to think about it often during our lifetime. We should contemplate its cause, which is sin, and its consequence, which is hell. We must not consider these in their own right, but always as they have been conquered by Christ.

Luther wrote, "We should familiarize ourselves with death during our lifetime, inviting death into our presence when it is still at a distance and not on the move. At the time of dying, however, this is hazardous and useless, for then death looms large of its own accord. In that hour we must put the thought of death out of mind and refuse to see it."

We pass our final test when we look through our dreaded enemy and focus solely on Jesus. Luther explained that we must use every tremble of sin, death, and hell as an excuse to run to Jesus. He said that Satan "makes our sins seem large and numerous. He reminds us . . . of the many who were damned for less sins than ours so as to make us despair or die reluctantly, thus forgetting God and being found disobedient in the hour of death." But if we run to the cross, we see that our sins "are overcome and swallowed up in Christ. He takes your death upon himself and strangles it so that it may not harm you."

You cannot beat
death, but you
know someone
who has.

You cannot beat death, but you know someone who has. Rest in Jesus, the God who shared your humanity so He might destroy death from the inside out. Curl up and go to sleep on the promises of God, knowing that the Father who raised

His Son from the dead will not leave you to languish in your grave. Rest in peace, for as good as life was this time around, it will be indescribably better when you return with Jesus.

You are going to die. Take a moment to let that sink in. You are going to *die*. Death is the final enemy you will ever face, and Satan has saved his largest scare for last. But fear is no match for faith. Do you believe that Jesus swam the sea of death, scattered "the king of terrors" (Job 18:14), and has now returned for you? Then climb on His back, and He will carry you. Here comes the fight of your life. Prepare to win.

Questions for Reflection

1. Why is your moment of death your ultimate test?

2. Why is it essential that you prepare for that test now, while it is still some distance away?

3. What should you think about death, and how should these beliefs inform what you feel as you prepare for it?

4. How is it a blessing to know that your time of death is near?

SOURCES

Chapter 1: Shock

Jean Gerson wrote *The Art of Dying*, Robert Bellarmine wrote *The Art of Dying Well*, and Erasmus wrote *Preparing for Death*.

Chapter 2: Focus

Matt Chandler's story can be found online: "Matt Chandler on Suffering," July 24, 2010, http://thegospelcoalition .org/blogs/justintaylor/2010/07/24/matt-chandler-on -suffering/; "One Year Later: An Interview with Matt Chandler," by Justin Taylor, November 1, 2010, http:// thegospelcoalition.org/blogs/justintaylor/2010/11/01/ one-year-later-an-interview-with-matt-chandler/; and Associated Press, "Brain Cancer Tests a Young Pastor's Faith," MSNBC.com, January 31, 2010, http://www.msnbc.msn .com/id/35086396/ns/health-cancer#.

John Calvin's words on providence appear in his *Institutes of the Christian Religion*, I.17.10.

William Faulkner, quoted in William P. Tuck, *Facing Grief and Death* (Nashville: Broadman Press, 1975), 75.

Chapter 3: Judgment

John Calvin's description of hell comes from his *Institutes of the Christian Religion*, III.25.12.

Chapter 4: Fear

Socrates's death is described in "The Suicide of Socrates, 399 B.C.," EyeWitness to History, 2003, http://www .eyewitnesstohistory.com/socrates.htm.

Augustine's quote comes from Sermon 348, 3, and appears in Donald X. Burt, *Reflections on a Dying Life* (Collegeville, MN: Liturgical Press, 2004), 127.

William Shakespeare, *Hamlet*, act 3, scene 1, as quoted in Richard Wolff, *The Last Enemy* (Washington, D.C.: Canon Press, 1974), 18.

Chapter 6: Sorrow

Christopher Hitchens's interview can be accessed online: "Christopher Hitchens: I'm Dying," interview by Jeffrey Goldberg, *Huffington Post*, August 10, 2010, updated March 23, 2011, http://www.huffingtonpost .com/2010/08/10/christopher-hitchens-im-d_n_676681 .html; "Christopher Hitchens on Cancer: I'm 'Realistic' about Odds of Survival, Pray for Me If You Want," *Huffington Post*, August 6, 2010, updated October 6, 2010, http://www.huffingtonpost.com/2010/08/06/ christopher-hitchens-on-c_n_673144.html.

The description of John Calvin's death is found in Bruce Gordon, *Calvin* (Yale University Press, 2009), 333–35.

Chapter 8: Sin

Mitch Albom, *Tuesdays with Morrie* (New York: Doubleday), 172–74.

Buddha's words on death can be read at http://www .buddhamind.info/leftside/under/buddha/b-life.htm.

Yoda's quote appears at http://thinkexist.com/quotes/like/ death-is-a-natural-part-of-life-rejoice-for-those/357218/.

Richard Dawkins, *The God Delusion* (New York: Houghton Mifflin Company, 2006), 357.

T. S. Eliot, "The Cocktail Party," as quoted in Peter Kreeft, *Love Is Stronger than Death* (San Francisco: Ignatius Press, 1992), 16.

Chapter 9: Guilt

"Slow Code," *All Things Considered*, NPR, February 11, 1998, available at http://www.npr.org/programs/death/980211 .death.html.

Martin Luther, "Table Talk," in *Luther's Works,* ed. and trans. Theodore G. Tappert, gen. ed. Helmut T. Lehmann (Philadelphia: Fortress Press, 1967), 54:65.

Ray S. Anderson, *Theology, Death and Dying* (New York: Basil Blackwell, 1986), 86.

Chapter 10: Enemy

Canon Henry Scott-Holland's poem belongs to his sermon "The King of Terrors" and is available online at http://www.poeticexpressions.co.uk/POEMS/Death%20 is%20nothing%20at%20all%20-%20Canon%20 Henry%20Scott-Holland.htm.

"The Conversion of Kübler-Ross," *Time*, November 12, 1979, 81. Quoted in Christopher P. Vogt, *Patience, Compassion, Hope, and the Christian Art of Dying Well* (New York: Sheed & Ward, 2004), 79.

Chapter 11: Crucifixion

Immaculée Ilibagiza, *Left to Tell: Discovering God Amidst the Rwandan Holocaust* (New York: Hay House, 2006).

W. S. Merwin, "For the Anniversary of My Death" from *The Second Four Books of Poems* (Port Townsend, WA: Copper Canyon Press, 1993), 115.

C. S. Lewis, *The Lion, the Witch, and the Wardrobe* (San Francisco: Harper Trophy, 2000), 163.

Chapter 12: Resurrection

Marcus J. Borg and N. T. Wright, *The Meaning of Jesus: Two Visions* (San Francisco: HarperCollins, 1999).

As reported in the *Grand Rapids Press*, April 8, 2006, D9, a Scripps Howard/Ohio University poll surveyed 1,007 adults and found that only 44 percent of Protestants and 59 percent of "born again" Americans said yes to the question, "Do you believe that, after you die, your physical body will be resurrected someday?"

Chapter 13: Triumph

Polycarp's story appears in J. Stevenson, ed., *A New Eusebius* (Cambridge, U.K.: SPCK Press, 1987), 23–30.

Ignatius's quotes are found in Henry Bettenson, ed., *The Early Christian Fathers* (New York: Oxford University Press, 1956), 45–46.

Martin Luther, quoted in Helmut Thielicke, *Living with Death* (Grand Rapids: Eerdmans, 1983), 191.

Chapter 14: Rest

Ed Dobson, *Prayers & Promises When Facing a Life-Threatening Illness* (Grand Rapids: Zondervan, 2007), 32–33.

Chapter 15: Repent

Karl Barth, *The Doctrine of Reconciliation*, vol. 4, part 1 of *Church Dogmatics*, ed. G. W. Bromiley and T. F. Torrance (Edinburgh: T. & T. Clark, 1957), 295.

Chapter 16: Hope

Nick Schuyler and Jeré Longman, *Not Without Hope* (New York: William Morrow, 2010).

Chapter 17: Heaven

Don Piper, *90 Minutes in Heaven* (Grand Rapids: Revell, 2004); Kevin Malarkey and Alex Malarkey, *The Boy Who Came Back from Heaven* (Carol Stream, IL: Tyndale, 2010); Todd Burpo, *Heaven Is for Real: A Little Boy's Astounding Story of His Trip to Heaven and Back* (Nashville: Thomas Nelson, 2010); Bill Wiese, *23 Minutes in Hell* (Lake Mary, FL: Charisma House, 2006).

Quotes from Origen, Gregory, Thérèse of Lisieux, and Martin Luther appear in Donald Bloesch, *The Last Things* (Downers Grove, IL: InterVarsity Press, 2004), 156, 170–71.

Chapter 18: Earth

For more on the cosmic scope of redemption and what we will do on the New Earth, see Michael Wittmer, *Heaven Is a Place on Earth* (Grand Rapids: Zondervan, 2004).

Chapter 19: More

Augustine, "On Rebuke and Grace," chap. 33, in Philip Schaff, ed., *A Select Library of the Nicene and Post-Nicene Fathers of the Christian Church,* first series, vol. 5 (1872; reprinted, Edinburgh: T. & T. Clark; Grand Rapids: Eerdmans, 1991), 485.

Chapter 20: Lament

John Piper, "Don't Waste Your Cancer," February 15, 2006, http://www.desiringgod.org/resource-library/taste-see-articles/dont-waste-your-cancer.

The translation of Question 1 of the Heidelberg Catechism comes from *Ecumenical Creeds and Reformed Confessions* (Grand Rapids: CRC Publications, 1988), 13.

Chapter 23: Finish Well

Heiko A. Oberman, *Luther: Man Between God and the Devil* (1982; New York: Image Books, 1992), 3–8.

Willie Nelson is quoted in Dotson Rader, "Three Chords and the Truth—That's What a Country Song Is," *Parade* (June 27, 2010): 5.

Martin Luther, "A Sermon on Preparing to Die," in *Martin Luther's Basic Theological Writings,* 2nd ed., ed. Timothy F. Lull (Minneapolis: Fortress Press, 2005), 418–28.

NOTE TO
THE READER

ABOUT THE AUTHOR

AN OHIO NATIVE (and demoralized fan of Cleveland sports teams), Mike attended seminary in Grand Rapids, where he has been stuck ever since. He isn't complaining, for West Michigan's many churches and miles of fresh water coastline make for a fine place to raise a family. He and his wife, Julie, have three young children, Avery, Landon, and Alayna. Because of them, he has no hobbies.

When Mike isn't playing catch or kick the can with his kids, he can be found teaching theology at Grand Rapids Theological Seminary. He also enjoys writing books, such as this one, that help Christians to treasure and apply the gospel to their lives. Nothing is more important, for we're all going to die. And then we live again!